1,000
Marbles

1,000 Marbles

A Little Something About Precious Time

Jeffrey Davis

**Andrews McMeel
Publishing**

Kansas City

01 02 03 04 05 RDC 10 9 8 7 6 5 4 3 2 1

Library of Congress Cataloging-in-Publication Data
Davis, Jeff, 1959–
    1,000 marbles : a little something about precious time / Jeff Davis.
        p. cm.
    ISBN 0-7407-1553-4 (pbk.)
        1. Conduct of life—Miscellanea. I. Title: One thousand marbles. II. Title.

BJ1595 .D355 2001
796.2—dc21

                                                            2001022647

Book design by Holly Camerlinck

This book is lovingly dedicated to my mom and dad,
who were the best parents a child could hope for
and the best friends a son could pray for.

Preface

*For what is your life? It is even a vapor that appears
for a little time and then vanishes away.*

—James 4:14

A strange thing happens if you live long enough—you get older. It first becomes noticeable when it seems you just took the Christmas tree down and suddenly it's the Fourth of July! Time seems to move faster and eventually there comes a point when you realize that even if you are very fortunate, your life is more than half over. Childhood dreams of being an astronaut, professional ballplayer, and president of the United States have slipped away.

Most of us spend five or more days a week earning a living, and there never seems to be enough time to do those things that we enjoy. Weekends and the occasional day off have become a precious thing. But without some advance thought and planning it's easy to let that time go to waste. And believe me, we never have enough time to waste.

That we are finite creatures with limited time to enjoy life isn't sad or unfair, but it does present for each and every one of us a choice. We can choose to squander our portion or we can make the most of it. I wrote "A Thousand Marbles" as a parable, to encourage my ham radio friends around the world to think about these things, consider their priorities, and make the most of whatever time they have left.

Imagine my surprise to find that the story has been re-told on over ten thousand Web sites and in countless e-mails across the Internet. I'm pleased that so many people found the story touching, but I'd be even happier if it changes just a few lives.

Many people receive good advice and ignore it. I trust you will receive it in the spirit it is given and value the "marbles" that you have remaining.

Acknowledgments

Following the story are a thousand suggestions—I call them marbles—of things to do on your days off. They aren't particularly profound, but they are some of the things that my friends and family find enjoyable. Some are written from their perspective, so if you see a "my husband and I" alongside a "my wife and I," that's why.

To those family, friends, and friends of friends, here's a very big thank-you. It is absolutely true that I never could have written this book without your help and inspiration. Believe me, writing a book takes several marbles, and many of you contributed at least one marble of your own when you took the time to share your thoughts. I hope you find it was time well spent. Thank you.

A Thousand Marbles

The older I get, the more I enjoy Saturday mornings. Perhaps it's the quiet solitude that comes with being the first to rise, or maybe it's the unbounded joy of not having to be at work. Either way, the first few hours of a Saturday morning are most enjoyable.

A few weeks ago, I was shuffling toward the basement with a steaming cup of coffee in one hand and the morning paper in the other. What began as a typical Saturday morning turned into one of those lessons that life seems to hand you from time to time. Let me tell you about it.

I settled behind my desk of radio equipment. Being a ham radio operator for over twenty years, I've accumulated a lot of it. I flipped the main switch that powers all of the equipment and waited patiently for the receiver to warm up.

I turned the dial up into the phone portion of the band in order to listen to a Saturday morning swap net. Along the way, I came across an older-sounding chap with a tremendous signal and a golden voice. You know the kind; he sounded like he should be in the broadcasting business. He was telling whomever he was talking with something about "a thousand marbles." I was intrigued and stopped to listen to what he had to say.

"Well, Tom, it sure sounds like you're busy with your job," he said. "I'm sure they pay you well, but it's a shame you have to be away from home and your family so much. Hard to believe a young fellow should have to work sixty or seventy hours a week to make ends meet. Too bad you missed your daughter's dance recital."

He continued, "Let me tell you something, Tom, something that has helped me keep a good perspective on my own priorities."

And that's when he began to explain his theory of a "thousand marbles."

"You see, I sat down one day and did a little arithmetic," he said. "The average person lives about seventy-five years. I know, some live more and some live less, but on average, folks live about seventy-five years.

"Now then, I multiplied seventy-five times fifty-two and I came up with 3,900, which is the number of Saturdays that the average person has in their entire lifetime. Now stick with me, Tom; I'm getting to the important part."

By this point, I was completely hooked on this conversation. Forget the swap net; I wasn't moving from this frequency until I heard what the old man had to say.

"It took me until I was fifty-five years old to think about all this in any detail," he went on, "and by that time I had lived through over 2,800 Saturdays. I got to thinking that if I lived to be seventy-five, I only had about a thousand of them left to enjoy.

"So I went to a toy store and bought every single marble they had. I ended up having to visit three stores to round up a thousand marbles. I took them home and put them inside of a large, clear plastic container right here in the room next to my radios. Every Saturday since then, I have taken one marble out and thrown it away.

"I found that by watching the marbles diminish, I focused more on the really important things in life. There is nothing like watching your time here on this earth run out to help get your priorities straight.

"Now let me tell you one last thing before I sign off with you and take my lovely wife out for breakfast. This morning, I took the very last marble out of the container. I figure that if I make it until next Saturday, then I've been given a little extra time. And the one thing we can all use is a little more time.

"It was nice to meet you, Tom. I hope you spend more time with your family, and I hope to meet you again here on the band. 73 Old Man, this is K9NZQ, clear and shutting down. Good morning!"

You could have heard a pin drop on the band when that fellow signed off. I guess he gave us all a lot to think about. I had planned to work on my antenna that morning, and then

I was going to meet up with a few local hams to work on the next club newsletter.

Instead, I went upstairs and woke my wife up with a kiss. "C'mon, honey, I'm taking you and the kids to breakfast."

"What brought this on?" she asked with a smile.

"Oh, nothing special. It's just been a long time since we spent a Saturday together with the kids. Hey, can we stop at a toy store while we're out? I need to buy some marbles."

1,000
Marbles

Learn the lyrics to a song whose tune has been stuck in your head for days.

*

Take a first aid and CPR class with your entire family. It could be one of the most valuable things that you ever do.

*

Learn enough astronomy to be able to point out various constellations and visible planets on a clear winter night.

*

Buy a book about paper airplane design and challenge your kids to see how many different kinds they can make and fly.

*

With your entire family, spend an afternoon designing a family crest. When complete, have the artwork transferred to shirts for everyone.

*

The kids *never* object to a trip to the local children's museum. Try it today.

The task of fixing a small dent or removing a rust spot on your car is best suited for two. It's a perfect opportunity for a long talk with a teenager as well as a great time to praise his or her hard work.

Find a book about kite construction and try your hand at making a unique design. Of course, it isn't really an official kite until you fly it!

On a cool Saturday evening we like to make a big pot of chili and corn muffins and invite the next-door neighbors over for a casual dinner.

Next time you see a hot air balloon in flight, give chase and see if you can find where it lands.

Everyone should have a place on the refrigerator with telephone numbers for your doctors, schools, workplace, pharmacist, and veterinarian. Take the time to make or update yours today.

It isn't necessarily fun, but it is the duty of every parent or grandparent to take a child to a Chuck E. Cheese at least once in his or her lifetime.

•

Make a trip to an art museum and study those things that are considered to be "art." In some instances, you might disagree with that assessment, and that's all right.

•

Join your neighborhood crime watch or start one if it doesn't already exist.

•

Organize a community clean-up day when you and your neighbors pick up trash, plant flowers, and beautify common areas around where you live.

•

Take flowers to someone you know who lives in a nursing home. Plan to spend a few hours visiting with him or her while you are there.

I like to take solitary walks in the woods during a gentle summer rain.

•

Buy a bottle of that stuff that makes your windshield easier to see out of when it rains. Spend the morning visiting several of your friends and relatives and apply it to their windshields. It's a good excuse to enjoy a short visit and one that will be appreciated.

•

Today would be a gooc day to take that wristwatch that stopped working months ago to the jewelry shop for repair.

•

Enjoy a breakfast muffin and coffee in the park early one Saturday morning before taking a long walk.

•

Spend the day building one of those model ships in a bottle—then send me a note and let me know how you did it!

I like to visit fancy furniture stores and make mental decorating plans. It doesn't cost a dime and if my ship ever comes in, I know how I'll decorate the mansion!

•

It doesn't matter if it's a swing set, a tire on a rope, or a fancy glider, no house is a "home" without a swing of some kind. If you don't have one, shop for one today.

•

Visit a candle shop to find a scented candle to set the perfect mood for a very special occasion.

•

The First Amendment can always use a little exercise. Write a letter to the editor of your paper about something about which you are passionate.

•

If you've never made a fire evacuation plan for your house, today would be a great time to make one and then practice it with your entire family.

Today would be a good one to have your fire extinguishers recharged and your smoke detector batteries replaced.

•

I love the automatic teller machine as much as the next person, but every now and again you should make an actual visit inside your bank to find out what's new. There could be a new service of which you aren't aware that would save you time or money.

•

Have breakfast with your insurance agent on occasion to review your policies and make sure that your coverage remains adequate for your present situation. Enjoy the time spent, as your agent is an important member of your financial success team.

•

On your next trip to the beach, take along a snorkel, mask, and fins, and enjoy a close-up view of the underwater world.

If you are like me, when you need an umbrella you can't find one. Why not buy an umbrella for your car today and keep it there.

●

Take a photography class and learn to take great pictures.

●

Learn to develop your own film and set up a dark room in your house.

●

Buy a couple of gallons of windshield washer fluid for your car. Use one for your own car but take the other to your parents' house and replenish their fluid too.

●

Make a long-distance call to a relative or friend and spend an hour chitchatting about nothing in particular. It costs less than a hamburger and fries but is worth more than all the fast food you can eat.

Make a batch of cookies with the help of your children or grandchildren, and take plenty of photographs of the event.

Very often a local factory will stage an "open house," allowing visitors a chance to view the manufacturing process close-up. If you get the chance, I'd recommend going. It's usually a lot of fun and modern automation can be a real kick to watch!

Take a calligraphy class, and next Christmas sign all your cards like a real John Hancock.

We save our newspapers until the pile has grown high. Then, on Saturday morning I load them up and take them to the local Boy Scouts, who recycle them to raise funds for their troop.

Find that book that you enjoyed so much as a youngster and read it to your own children—or just read it again for your own enjoyment.

Attend a town council meeting one Saturday, just to see for yourself what goes on there.

Spend one morning in December decorating the trees in your yard with Christmas lights just like you always planned to do but never got around to doing.

You can probably think of a special dish that you or a relative makes that is unique, something you can't get at any restaurant. You need to put that recipe on paper so that your family can enjoy it for generations to come.

Visit an air show if you ever get the chance. You'll be amazed at what flying machines can do.

Make it your mission this Saturday to fix every VCR display in your home so that you never have to see the dreaded flashing 12:00 A.M. again!

Throw a forties bash at your house this Saturday night. Put on the big band music of Glenn Miller and Artie Shaw. Then move the coffee table out of the way to make room for the Lindy Hop.

The next time you go to the grocery, spend a little time looking at the community bulletin board. You could find a baby-sitter, free kitten, or a good deal on a chain saw.

I've got myself on a mailing list for lectures that take place at a state college in my hometown. While I don't care for all of them, there are many interesting lectures to be enjoyed. Find out what's available in your area and give it a try.

A little wild birdseed and a properly placed feeder will bring you years of bird-watching enjoyment from your kitchen window.

●

Make sure you shop for a new window scraper for your car *before* winter weather sets in. Today would be a good day to buy one to use and one to give to a friend.

●

Attend your local soapbox derby this year. It could be all the inspiration your daughter needs to enter the contest next year.

●

Host a very fancy, dress-up tea party for your daughter or granddaughter.

●

Find a recipe for potato pancakes and, after you've practiced making them a few times, invite some close friends over for a special breakfast featuring your potato pancakes.

I enjoy visiting large home-improvement stores and viewing the new kitchen countertops, cabinets, interior French doors, and riding lawn mowers that I will probably never get around to buying.

Spend time planting an abundance of mums all over your yard, and in the fall, when the trees begin to lose their grasp on the leaves, your yard will be a canvas filled with color.

Learn a few words and phrases using sign language. You never know when it will come in handy.

Grow your own alfalfa sprouts in your kitchen window and you'll never be without a fresh topping for your salad.

Spend the afternoon playing with a puppy—even if you have to borrow one.

Making your own address sign for your house is an afternoon workshop project that will make you smile.

Plan an overnight stay at a bed-and-breakfast and enjoy the warm, cozy amenities.

Create your own Web page and use it as a place to post recent photos and a journal of your travels so that no matter where they live, your family can follow your adventures.

Research several recipes and spend time in the kitchen experimenting until you come up with a killer pumpkin pie. Don't be happy until it's so good friends ask you for the recipe.

Uncle Norman and Aunt Edith love to play bingo once a week at the local Wal-Mart. The friends they have made there make it time well spent.

Many years ago at summer camp I took archery lessons. I really enjoyed doing that. I think one day I will find a way to do that again.

Being a full-time mother does not give me much time for yoga or tai chi, but there are a few things that I do to relax. I turn all the phones off, and I sit in the middle of the family room on the floor and let my children run amuck. I watch and enjoy. Smiling and belly laughing are so relaxing. If I have paperwork to take care of, like a script to read, I sneak away to my favorite café for an hour or so and enjoy an excellent cup of tomato basil soup or a cup of French coffee and a pastry while I read.

—Nia Peeples, actress

Spend a rainy afternoon calculating the actual odds of your winning the lottery, and there's a good chance you'll never play it again.

•

Install a badminton or volleyball net in your backyard. The next time you have friends over and they bring their children, you'll be their hero for a day.

•

Find a pen pal in another country. It's downright easy to do via e-mail these days. The cultural exchange is well worth the effort, and who knows, you might make a lifelong friend.

•

Don't believe the bunk that you are too old to learn to do anything. If you've always wanted to play a musical instrument, make the arrangements and take the first lesson you can book. What do you have to lose?

•

You can sample the food from dozens of restaurants in a single afternoon at a Taste of Cincinnati or similar festival.

In the spring, church leagues are always looking for volunteers to play softball. Here's your chance to look good in a uniform and nobody will laugh at you for striking out.

•

Make it a family project to install a flagpole surrounded by flowers in your yard. You'll be glad you did on Flag Day!

•

Take your sweetie to a karaoke night event and showcase your talent—or lack thereof. You'll look good even if you sound bad.

•

Spend the afternoon with your friends watching a college football game on the big screen at a local sports bar.

•

Take a long walk around your neighborhood hand in hand with someone you love. Agree before you leave that neither of you will say a single word for the entire walk.

If the two of you haven't been out for quite some time, make plans to go dancing tonight. One good evening of dinner and dancing makes up for a lot of late nights stuck at the office.

•

Find a book or Web site that explains how to host a "Who Done It?" party. With it all set up, have your friends over for an evening of mystery and intrigue.

•

Get up very early one Saturday morning and have your oil changed, tires rotated, and car washed before 11 A.M. You'll be amazed at how good you will feel having accomplished so much and still have nearly the entire day in front of you.

•

Have you ever made anything with needlepoint? I haven't, but I've watched my wife do it and I'd trade a marble to learn that skill.

It can take a long time to make your very own quilt, but the end result is well worth the effort. Spend a few hours quilting when the weather is bad and before you know it, you'll be enjoying your own handmade quilt.

It might require a road trip, but everyone should have a picture of him- or herself standing next to a Route 66 road sign.

If you don't have a basketball goal at your house, hop on your bike and ride over to a neighborhood school that has a court.

Purchase plastic molds, paper sticks, and the ingredients so you can make your own lollipops on a cold winter afternoon.

One rainy Saturday afternoon take a ball of string, a box of macaroni, and some spray paint into the garage with your daughter. Don't come out until you have macaroni necklaces for everyone.

Visit a craft store with your children or grandchildren and let them pick out a project that you can take home and work on together. Don't forget to snap a few pictures!

You'll never survive in the wild if you don't know how to start a campfire. Do a little research and learn to build a campfire today!

Join a book club and attend meetings in or around your town. Reviewing books with others can be an eye-opening experience.

Attend an African Folk Tale Festival that features storytellers and musicians as they tell stories through song and dance. Enjoy this special treat with someone you love.

In the fall we always enjoy a visit to a harvest celebration that presents Native food sources, authentic Native American meals, and live entertainment.

Find a venue for a local film festival where you can recognize filmmakers whose work explores the human journey by artistically expressing hope and respect for the positive values of life.

•

Attend a local art festival. The artists appreciate your support, and you may even find a gem for one of your walls.

•

If you are a budding shutterbug, refine your craft and share your images with like-minded photography buffs by joining a camera club.

•

I once attended the ninetieth anniversary celebration at a Greek Orthodox Church. The architecture was stunning and the event was very enjoyable. Since then, I always look for similar opportunities and gladly exchange a marble for such pleasure.

Spend the afternoon at a winery enjoying a tasting event and tour.

•

Create a family chain letter, where you write something and then mail it to a relative. She adds to your letter and sends it to another, and so on.

•

On a Saturday evening during the Christmas season, find the closest place where you can enjoy a live performance of *The Nutcracker.*

•

Take a drive through a live nativity scene this holiday season.

•

Organize a baby shower for an expecting friend, coworker, or relative.

•

Throw a bridal shower for a soon to be married friend, coworker, or relative.

Organize a surprise birthday party for one of your parents. It would be a wonderful touch if you could arrange to have one of their long-lost friends attend as a special surprise.

Spend time today to make plans for a party celebrating a major anniversary milestone (thirtieth, fortieth, or fiftieth anniversary) for your parents or grandparents.

Make a videotape of your house, carefully including the inside and out. It could prove invaluable for your insurance should disaster ever strike.

Spend the morning shopping for new shoes. Top it off with lunch at your favorite place.

Enjoy a fancy picnic in the park complete with basket, flatware, and blanket. Even if no one else goes along, the ants will be happy to attend!

Attending an outdoors jazz festival is one of those
things you do that you'll always remember with a
warm smile.

After a crazy week when nothing seems to go your way,
you deserve a nice long bubble bath with your favorite
magazine and a few scented candles. Don't forget to turn
off the ringer on the phone.

You'll be proud to show off your handiwork when you
make your very own candles. You can't really go
wrong since you can always burn the evidence.

Try your hand at creating your own decorative centerpiece.
It most certainly will be a conversation starter at dinner.

We are fortunate that old-time radio broadcasts are
still available on cassette. I like to listen to old Fibber
McGee and Jack Armstrong radio shows and have a
growing collection of them on tape.

Try your hand at basket weaving. You might even want to take a class. I was surprised to find so many people who enjoy this unique hobby.

•

Making your own Christmas wreath is the only way to get exactly what you want. It's also a perfect project for two.

•

From time to time I've found it useful to commit both long- and short-term life goals to paper. Writing your specific goals on paper causes you to think specifically about what you want to achieve, and that somehow moves them closer to reality.

•

It's a worthwhile exercise to write down the biggest problems that you currently face. A year from now you'll likely chuckle as you review what little problems they actually were.

Prepare a time capsule with photos, newspaper clippings, modern music, and so on. Instruct your children or grandchildren to open it twenty years later and they will treasure what you have left for them.

Exploring your family tree is a bit easier these days with various online resources. You could be delighted or perhaps chagrined to find a distant relative who was a notorious criminal.

A few hours spent with a travel agent on a cold winter day could warm your spirits. It could also put cruise tickets in your pocket, so beware!

A handmade teddy bear is a cherished gift for anyone and for any occasion. Begin to make one today.

I like to visit a large greenhouse in the winter. While the cold winds blow outside, the plants inside bask in warmth and light.

Attending an investment club meeting is the best way to find out if you would like to join.

•

Sometimes you have to go a little crazy. Go ahead, I dare you. Change your hair color *radically* today.

•

Spend the day visiting several health clubs and spas in your area until you find the perfect one for you to join. Promise yourself that no matter what, you won't join until a week has passed. You'll always make better decisions after a few days to think it over.

•

A special breakfast requires extra planning. Think about an egg quiche with fresh strawberries and mimosas served on the patio under a glorious blue-sky morning.

•

Spend a few hours with a good book, sitting as far in the back as you can possibly get at a quiet coffeehouse.

can think of no hobby more rewarding than ancestor hunting. My most fun search is going into courthouses and finding documents about a great-grandparent that of course died a hundred or two hundred years ago. Even more exciting is to find a cemetery marker for one born in 1703 or 1727, as I did in North Carolina, that was very readable, or to go to Ireland and meet family by the same name and find that they resemble us. I want my grandchildren to know their roots if they are ever interested. Very few people are until it is too late to ask living relatives. I was luckier than most because my mother lived to be 104 years of age with a mind clearer than mine now. So for several years I have spent time researching family—my husband's family first, since we live in his home community, and now my mother's and my father's families. I know no one will ever go through my files, so I am trying to get it all down in print.

—Margaret Adams, grandmother

Never miss the chance to take your shoes and socks off, roll up your pants, and go wading in a stream.

Invite your mother to lunch. Take her someplace that's very nice and enjoy a leisurely visit. You'll know you've been there long enough when after dessert the waitperson has asked you for the third time if you "care for anything else?"

Spend the afternoon shopping for a new dress that is one size too small as an added incentive to lose a few pounds.

When you need to have a long talk with a close friend, try to have it while tossing a Frisbee back and forth in the warm sunshine. There isn't much you can't work out that way.

Volunteer to distribute your church flyers at hotels and motels around town. Folks just passing through town may decide to worship with you.

One of life's more enjoyable indulgences is time spent in a steamy outdoor hot tub while snow is falling all around you.

A lazy, hot summer afternoon is a good time to be thankful for air-conditioning while you enjoy your stamp collection.

Once a month, whether I need it or not, I like to go to a *real* barbershop. I'm not talking about a *salon;* I'm talking two chairs, no waiting. It must have a liberal supply of outdoor and sporting magazines to peruse and a soda machine that doesn't make change to be considered a *real* barbershop.

Look for a public auto auction to attend. You might be surprised at the deals you can find, but remember, if it looks too good to be true, it probably is!

Sitting atop eighteen inches of frozen water with a biting cold wind in your face seems pointless until there's a tug on the line that disappears into the frozen abyss. Ice fishing requires an abundance of faith that life goes on despite evidence to the contrary.

Volunteer to work for the campaign of a candidate whom you admire. Being active in the political process is an important civic duty that you shouldn't neglect.

Standing in a river trying to convince rainbow trout to fall for your little deception is a pretty good way to forget your troubles, if you ask me.

Check the maps, decide on the route, and gather everything that you will need, then set out on a long, cross-country ride on your bicycle.

I've found that attending a poetry reading is always a fifty-fifty proposition. It is either very good or very bad. Give it a try and see if you agree.

●

I've never met anyone who didn't know how to swim who didn't say they wished they had learned to swim when they were young. So here is your chance to be young again: Take swimming lessons.

●

You really can't learn to play golf by yourself. Begin to take lessons this week and before you know it, you'll be hitting the ball in the water as well as seasoned veterans.

●

The holiday season isn't "official" until you take the children to have their pictures taken with Santa Claus.

I can't even begin to explain what a rabbit has to do with Easter, but your collection of family photos isn't complete without a shot of the children with the Easter Bunny.

•

Visiting an antique bookstore will make you acutely aware that sometimes, the book is more valuable than the story it contains.

•

Visit a public aquarium and enjoy the bizarre-looking creatures that call the deep home.

•

Attend one of those seminars that claim to show you how to become a millionaire overnight. Once you've seen it you'll never have to wonder about them again. On the other hand, if you actually become a millionaire from attending one, then I'm sure you'll want to reward a certain writer who suggested this idea to begin with!

Set up a tent in the backyard for a few days and let the kids camp out without ever leaving your yard.

●

Rise very early one day and, after breakfast at your favorite place, spend the rest of the morning on a hunt for undervalued antiques.

●

Who wouldn't want to play a rousing game of "capture the flag" just after dark? It will be a big hit with the neighborhood kids.

●

The kids thought it was a great adventure when we attached their name and address to a helium balloon and let it go. It was even more fun to show folks the letter we got back from a fellow five hundred miles away who found that balloon in his yard.

●

Indoor paint ball is a legal way to shoot your best friend or spouse!

For reasons not totally understood, the kids enjoy playing laser tag at that noisy place in the mall. With them running like crazy inside, I like munching a hot pretzel while waiting for them to run out of gas.

●

There is just about no end to what you can do with an old milk can once you've decorated and dressed it up a bit. Find one at a rummage sale and see what you can do with yours.

●

Decorating cookies with the children is a pretty good excuse for abandoning your diet—at least for one day.

●

I've never taken a one-day bus trip with a group of people, but based on the loud laughter I've heard when a busload of people disembark at a restaurant, I'd have to guess it's a lot of fun.

Taking a cake-decorating class and having people heap praise on your edible works of art is an excellent use of a marble.

Most towns have an active astronomy club. Why not attend their next meeting and get in on the fun of skygazing? Staring into the heavens is something you have in common with your great-great-great-grandfather.

Visit a candy store and watch them dip the cherries into dark chocolate before you buy them.

Sending letters on stationery that you designed is very impressive because you actually took the time and made the effort to do it yourself.

Try your hand at origami, the Japanese art of folding paper to look like all sorts of living things.

The thrill that comes from indoor skydiving is the next best thing to stepping out of a perfectly good plane!

●

Today is the day to wallpaper a room or wall in your house to create the look that you want.

●

Collect old beaded jewelry from rummage sales and wherever else you can find it. Then on a rainy day, you and your daughter will enjoy restringing the beads to make custom jewelry!

●

Indoor rock climbing offers you a chance to break a few bones without all the expense and trouble of traveling to the mountains.

●

I like to find a shady spot at the beach where the sound and smell of the surf put me to sleep.

I need to do something physical. Scuba diving or long hikes in wilderness settings.

—Michael Crichton, author

I like to walk around downtown a few days before Christmas. The shops and streets are warmly decorated with lights and ornaments. Folks who wouldn't normally look you in the eye will wish you Merry Christmas, and for a short time, the world seems a little closer.

I like to go to the park to feed the pigeons. It's peaceful there. The birds ask for nothing but seem genuinely grateful to receive so little. We could learn a lot from the birds at the park.

Some evening after taking the dog for a walk, spend a few minutes observing the moon hanging above the horizon. It's amazing to think that your ancestors saw this exact same thing thousands of years before you were born.

Go to a renaissance festival and get in touch with your chivalrous side.

A grandfather and grandchild on a teeter-totter provides an unmatched family photo opportunity.

Visit historic Washington, D.C., without leaving your house. Videos abound that take you on fascinating tours of our nation's capital. Rent one today.

❋

Look for a garden show in your area where you can gather all the information you need to improve your own harvest of vegetables or flowers next year.

❋

Take a cooking class through a community college or culinary center and add to your growing culinary skills while making new friends at the same time.

❋

Almost everyone could use a little work on their public speaking and communications skills. Find a Toastmasters Club near you where you can hone your speaking skills in a supportive environment.

Tired of beating the same three people in chess every time you play? Enter a chess tournament and put your strategic skills to the test.

Take a child to a puppet show and watch them smile. If you can't find one, then put on your very own sock puppet show and watch them laugh!

After a week of toil in building a new nation, early American settlers would gather in the community center on Saturday evening and enjoy dancing their favorite Old World folk dances. That's how square dancing started, and hearty enthusiasts are still at it today. Why not join in on the fun?

From jeans to suits, slacks to dresses, anything really goes at a ballet. Wear whatever makes you feel comfortable. You're there to be entertained.

If laughter is good for the soul, then tonight might be a good one for dinner on the town and a visit to a comedy club.

Having designs airbrushed onto your fingernails is a nonpermanent way to explore the human canvas.

Pamper yourself with a visit to an image consultant and see what they suggest that will give you the look you desire.

Oktoberfest is one of the world's largest parties. The festival began in 1810 to celebrate a wedding and the party has never really ended. Look for a festival where you can enjoy the fun, food, and drink.

Learn to play backgammon well and you can always find a game at a local club or, if you prefer to stay home, on the Internet.

Take a self-defense course and learn the skills, strategies, and physical techniques that could enable you to escape, resist, and survive violent attacks.

Exercise your mind by taking a creative writing class. Keep in mind that you are doing this for fun and not a grade, so relax and enjoy it.

Take an evening drive through town and enjoy all the holiday lights and decorations during the Christmas season.

Have your small children write down what they would like to be or do when they are grown. Present that document to them when they graduate high school.

Attending a Disney on Ice show is something you and your children will never forget.

Schools and libraries often sponsor book fairs for children. Look for one to visit and enjoy the stories and squeals of delight from the kids.

Celebrate the magic of Christmas and build a gingerbread house. Be careful, though—it can easily become an annual tradition!

Join the festivities when your town lights up the big Christmas tree this year.

Finger painting can be more than "kid stuff" that belongs in the kindergarten classroom and on the refrigerator door. Try it for yourself—you may discover something wonderful in the medium and in yourself as well.

Every child deserves to be read the story "Androcles and the Lion." Read it tonight before bed by candlelight.

It may sound like a summer camp project, but creating sand art is an enjoyable pastime for kids of all ages. Just pour different colors of sand in layers into a glass bottle.

●

Try your hand at the art of pressed flowers. They bring the beauty of the outdoors inside and make a very distinctive and thoughtful gift for your friends.

●

A good magic show is more of a production than most small-time theater. Watch your newspaper for a local show and plan to attend.

●

Wood carving is an old, much-loved, and practical art that you should really try. It's peaceful, relaxing, and the end result is a unique work of art by your own hand.

●

Put on old clothes and ride your bicycle after a rain shower. Don't miss those big puddles that splash up your back— that's half the fun!

Watching hockey on television is no way to enjoy the game. You have to attend to really appreciate the fast action on ice.

•

Over two hundred years ago British and other European observers commented on the American habit of whittling. Everybody whittled, from General Grant on down to the enlisted men. A pocketknife and a piece of wood are all you need to enjoy this age-old pastime.

•

Learn a few sleight-of-hand and card tricks for the kids and before long, you could find yourself the favorite uncle in the family.

•

Spend the day at the lanes improving your bowling game.

•

Treat yourself to a truly incomparable experience by dining at a five-star restaurant tonight. Don't forget to make reservations; you'll need them.

You don't have to wait for the Indianapolis 500 to enjoy motor sports. Small tracks have popped up all over the country and chances are good you can enjoy a night of Midget Auto Racing without having to travel too far to do it.

*

Feast on a sumptuous buffet and be entertained with a Broadway-style show by taking your date to a dinner theater this evening.

*

Try jumping a rope today. The activity is not just for kids anymore. It's good exercise and lots of fun. How many skipping-rope rhymes do you know?

*

After a particularly tough week at the salt mine, maybe today would be a good one to sleep late and catch up on your rest. You have to plan a day like this though: Be sure to rent a movie and have a good book on hand so you can spend the entire day in lounge mode.

Many people who have experienced fire walking feel that they can attain virtually any goal. I've never done it myself, but I have reserved a marble to learn more about it.

●

Spend the afternoon at a model railroad show. You could be bitten by the bug and decide this is a hobby for you.

●

In the mad rush to convenience we have forgotten many of the old ways, one of these being the simple art of soap making. Making a useful product with your very own hands is not only pleasurable, but also practical. How many people do you know who make their very own soap? Find out more about this intriguing hobby and give it a try!

●

Attending a conference is a great way to learn about something that interests you. It's also a wonderful way to meet and network with others who share your interests.

Hand spinning is the nearly forgotten process of taking natural material that is peacefully given to us by fiber-bearing animals and manipulating it into a product that is useful to humans. Spend the morning learning more about this craft.

A scarf or shawl that you hand weave yourself will be a gift that is treasured forever by the lucky person who receives it.

Determine to knit a sweater for yourself in the summer and you'll be ready for those cooler days ahead.

Take the time to handmake some of your very own holiday decorations. After just a few years of use these gain in personal value and become heirlooms for your children and grandchildren.

Spend the day shopping for an Oriental or Persian rug. Study your floor space and think about colors before you go.

Attend a one-day computer workshop to brush up on your operating system or application skills. The knowledge will make you more valuable where you work, and it could help you recover from the blue screen of death!

Nothing transforms a room like a hanging tapestry. It's definitely an Old World accruement. Spend an afternoon shopping for a reproduction that would restyle a room in your house.

As improbable as it may seem, there are people who not only collect laces, but also make their very own by hand. I've got to reserve a marble to find out more about this one day.

One of the more useful skills anyone can learn is basic sewing. No one should be far from home and unable to replace a button or add a quick stitch. Read a book, watch a video, or ask a seamstress to show you the basics. Then be sure to add an emergency sewing kit to your glove box or briefcase.

Almost everyone has dreamed of finding hidden treasure at one time or another. I was surprised to learn that there are a large number of groups and clubs that specialize in finding treasure. Break out your old metal detector and spend an afternoon looking for your own treasure.

You know that you've always wanted to do it, but you never thought you could learn. I'm telling you that you *can* learn to juggle, and you can begin this afternoon! Won't that look good on your résumé?

Join the ranks of scrapbooking enthusiasts and assemble some impressive memories to revisit many years from now. Find out more about it and then give it a try.

※

You pick up a book of matches from every special restaurant, resort, and hotel that you visit. Before you know it you have an impressive collection. Some matchbook collections are worth thousands of dollars. Do a little sleuthing and find out what yours may be worth today.

※

Boy Scouts learn to tie knots, and it can be a very useful skill. Find a Boy Scout today and have him show you all the basic knots. It will make him feel special and it will you, too!

※

A basement or garage isn't worth a dime if it doesn't have a dartboard. Install one and let the games begin!

This rainy afternoon looks like a good one for a visit to the local pub and a rousing game of Foosball.

·

Relive the exciting drama of the American Civil War by attending a reenactment of a specific battle. These events are complete with uniforms, handguns, and cannons typical of the period.

·

Buy your dad or grandfather a rain gauge and help him install it in his yard. It will give him hours of joy checking the rainfall amount. Don't ask me why; just trust me on this one.

·

Parchment craft is an old hobby that has found new popularity. You start with a thick, translucent sheet of parchment paper and end up with an elegant work of art. Find a book and learn all about it.

Literally thousands of restoration projects are going on at any one time. Almost all of them involve a large number of volunteers. If you find a particular project that interests you, then contact them and volunteer your services. You'll be glad you did.

•

Orienteering is a sport in which orienteers use an accurate, detailed map and a compass to find points in the landscape. It can be enjoyed as a walk in the woods or as a competitive sport. Join a local group and you may never get lost again!

•

Autumn in northern areas is a great time of the year to enjoy mountain biking. Along with the beautiful colors that are part of this pleasant seasonal change are many other benefits to getting out there on your fat-tired steed!

•

What better way to enjoy the gorgeous fall colors than on foot with a backpack? Be flexible and consult the hot lines to find out where the best colors are.

Rapelling down a minor cliff was a thrill a friend experienced as a Girl Scout. She'd like to try it again, and she recommends it to the adventurous.

You don't have to have a mountain to go rock climbing. City of Rocks in Idaho, for one, is a great place to start!

I will probably never try bungee jumping . . . but that doesn't mean that you shouldn't!

Take your daughter or granddaughter to an elegant lunch and a fashion show at the mall. It's quality time that you'll never regret.

I was driving through Eaton, Ohio, one Saturday afternoon and found myself in the middle of the largest pork festival in the country. It was worth a stop to enjoy a barbecue sandwich with thirty thousand pork enthusiasts.

Muster up your courage and enter your homemade chili in a contest.

•

Contact someone at your local high school and volunteer to chaperone at the prom or another dance. It will give you new insight into the youth culture and remind you of your own high school days.

•

If you live in an area that enjoys cold, hard winters, then you need to attend a winter festival. These are loud proclamations that we are a hearty people and not afraid of old man winter!

•

You know that killer pumpkin pie that you make and your friends say is the best they've ever had? Enter one of those in a pie contest and see if your friends are just being nice.

•

Make a "cheat sheet" with metric conversions for typical values that you can carry with you until you have memorized them.

Most people are ignorant of world geography. Buy a globe and spend a few hours getting acquainted with the world. Next time someone asks where the Maldives are, you can be the first to volunteer that information.

*

Spend an afternoon with the kids at a family fun center. Go-cart racing is always a big winner with the kids.

*

Did you know you could see the International Space Station with your naked eye? A number of Web sites and newspapers provide overhead pass information. Why not have some friends over on a clear evening when a pass is predicted for your area and see if you can find it?

*

Launch your own personal training regimen and plan to run in an upcoming 5K or 10K run for charity. No one loses and everyone wins.

I like to visit cookware stores. There is always some new doodad or gadget that makes it easier to slice eggs or butter toast and I never tire of adding them to my collection.

If you're like us, the cupboards soon fill with jelly jars and plastic promotional cups from fast food places. Once in a while you have to visit a glass factory outlet and buy a new collection of drinking glasses.

Volunteer to make cupcakes for a class party at a local elementary school.

Take an older relative or friend out for a birthday dinner at one of those places where they will sing "Happy Birthday" if you ask.

Look for a gospel sing in your area and make plans to attend.

Put up a free lemonade stand on a hot summer day when all your neighbors are busy working in their yard. You might make a new friend or two.

Share a marble—volunteer to work for a day on a Habitat for Humanity project in your city.

Nothing beats a horse-drawn carriage ride on a Saturday evening with someone you love.

Not long after my wife and I were first married, I lost my job. Money was tight, but we survived somehow on seventy-four dollars a week of unemployment. Dinner each evening was grilled cheese and tomato soup. Twenty years later, our cupboard isn't quite as bare, and yet from time to time, we still will have grilled cheese and tomato soup and talk about the "good old days." They seemed trying at the time, but now they've become treasured memories.

If you have never attended a dog show then you should!

In Cincinnati you can take a three-hour riverboat dinner cruise. A live band plays while the boat makes a leisurely trip up the river and back. The *Queen City* provides a majestic view from the river.

Sometimes we like to take a trip to a larger city and go shopping at a place where we have never been before.

At some point in your life, you should attend a major college football game. It's one of the very few ways you can ever realize just how many a hundred thousand people really are.

The Saturday after Thanksgiving is when we always kick off the "official" Christmas shopping season. After a long day at the mall those leftovers look pretty good.

The first good snowfall of the season is the best time to build a snow fort. Why do you need a fort, you ask? It provides the best protection from the snowball fight!

By the second good snowfall of the season you should have the snowball fight out of the way so you can spend more constructive time building a world-class snowman, complete with a top hat, scarf, button nose, and two eyes made out of coal.

Donate blood at your local hospital.

Surprise your husband by making all the arrangements so the two of you can go to an indoor tractor pull and truck show.

Spend a Saturday reviewing and organizing all of your personal insurance and other financial papers.

Write a letter to your children that won't be read until after your death.

•

No one likes to do it, but this Saturday determine to spend the day cleaning the basement.

•

AM broadcast radio signals travel farther at night. Try to see what's the most distant station you can pick up on your car radio while driving home some night.

•

Attending an indoor bicycle race can be enjoyable, but it's even _more_ fun to say the word "velodrome" when you tell people what you did last weekend!

•

It requires a little research and a lot of planning, but have a party at your house with a Hawaiian theme. The right food, music, and dress will make it a memorable occasion for you and your friends.

Take plenty of photos of your home and personal property and store the negatives in your safety deposit box. They could prove to be invaluable in the event of a fire or theft.

•

Spend the afternoon shopping for a small gift. Have it wrapped and take it to an elderly neighbor.

•

Follow a lazy stream for a while before having a sandwich on its friendly bank.

•

Gather your entire family together and visit a studio to have a family photo made.

•

Sometimes I like to read the *London Times* newspaper online.

Few people have the discipline to put all the phone numbers and addresses collected from friends and relatives over the years into their new computer. Spend time this Saturday doing just that.

●

The knowledge that winter is just around the corner usually hits me when I've mowed the lawn for the last time. Preparing the mower for winter, I drain the oil, replace the spark plug, and have the blade sharpened. After that, the mower is ready for a long winter rest.

●

Slicing a large, cold watermelon in your backyard on a hot summer day is sure to attract a crowd.

●

Most people have some old heirloom or antique in their home whose value is unknown. Spend a marble and visit with an expert to see if the value can be determined.

Get a little crazy and rearrange all of the pictures in your living room!

●

Visit a cyber café where you can enjoy a cup of coffee, check your e-mail, and surf the World Wide Web for a few dollars.

●

A snow-covered hill is an open invitation for sledding. When was the last time you went sliding down a hill astride a Flexible Flyer? Two hours of sledding followed by a cup of hot chocolate will hit the spot.

●

Cross-country snow skiing is a pursuit that doesn't require a lift, lodge, or even a mountain to enjoy.

●

How much fun can you have snow shoeing? You'll never know until you give it a try, but I can tell you it's a well-spent marble.

My favorite part of Thanksgiving is spending the whole day with family and friends. Why wait? Invite them over for an all-day party next weekend. Make sure everyone brings their favorite board game and a snack, and you'll be set.

Who wouldn't enjoy a visit to a water park on a hot summer day? The refreshing spray of cool water on a hot day makes everyone squeal with delight.

There is always an opportunity to go Christmas caroling with some group in your community. Try it some year; you'll be glad you did.

I didn't know what a luminary was until we moved to North Carolina some years ago. All of our neighbors asked if we were going on a luminary walk with them . . . so we did. The glow from hundreds of luminaries was a beautiful sight and added something special to the Christmas spirit that year.

I *have a little cottage up in British Columbia; I've had it since 1970. The last couple of years I had a weekly social event that kinda happened by accident. It was a potluck where people would drop by, and yeah, it was usually outside with candles and two strings of lights.*

**—Joni Mitchell,
singer and songwriter**

Those who never enjoyed art in primary school often find that taking an art class as an adult is a much more enjoyable endeavor. You can take a ceramics, painting, sculpting, and every other kind of art class in your spare time.

I've never been parasailing, but I've seen pictures of those who hang gracefully (and some not so gracefully) behind a boat over a body of water and it looks like fun. I have reserved a marble to give it a try.

Scuba diving requires special training and equipment, but it can provide a lifetime of enjoyment and an opportunity to enjoy the beauty of the deep.

For most of us, swimming with dolphins seems out of reach, yet those who actually do it speak so passionately about the experience that I'd love to trade a marble for the chance.

If you've never taken your lover ice skating you should make plans to spend a marble on ice.

●

Roller skating doesn't have to be a sport for youngsters. I hear that just putting on the skates makes you five years younger. Imagine how young you'll be after an entire afternoon on them.

●

Everyone looks silly in a batting cage. But take the kids and do it anyway. It's a lot of fun!

●

Golf doesn't always require a fairway. Miniature golf is a way to spend the afternoon getting to know your kids.

●

Playing tennis is a great workout. Just don't try to jump over the net when you win—especially if you just beat your wife or boss.

I live near a golf course and see people play in hot weather, cold weather, rain, and snow. It seems that golf lovers don't care about the weather, so what are you waiting for?

Some of our favorite family time is when the kids' friends come to our house and we play the board game Risk all night long with them. Total world domination is within your reach, but don't run out of food with a house full of teenagers!

I like going to the circus. Where else can you see elephants stand on one leg while a man walks a tightrope overhead?

Did you know that you can buy green coffee beans and roast your own coffee at home? Here's your chance to dazzle your friends with your very own blend of coffee.

Once in a while, gather up all the clothes that you no longer wear and donate them to Goodwill. Others will benefit and so will your overcrowded closet.

·

Touring selected neighborhoods during a Parade of Homes will give you plenty to dream about.

·

Our family likes to stay in a hotel with an indoor swimming pool once or twice during the winter. It's a nice break when the cold weather seems to drag on too long.

·

Taking a long hike in the woods on a beautiful day is almost guaranteed to make you appreciate the wonders of nature.

·

If patience is truly a virtue, then learning to tie a fly must be a holy act. But with the right tools, tying your own flies is not only possible, but it makes catching fish all the more enjoyable.

A flower garden is God's way of allowing you to create. Designing the layout and look of your own garden puts you in the same class as van Gogh without the easel or paint.

Where would we be without trees? Plan to spend one Saturday afternoon planting a tree on your property or in a park. The planet can use all the help you care to give it.

A trip to the beach wouldn't be complete without building a sandcastle.

Have you ever attended a bluegrass festival? It's impossible to listen to banjo music and not be happy.

My daughter would be happy if we spent an entire day at the beach doing nothing but collecting seashells.

Taking dance lessons is time well spent, especially when you consider it takes two to tango.

Have you ever built anything out of wood? Try it sometime. Build a birdhouse or a mailbox or just a number sign for your house. Creating something out of wood provides a great deal of personal pleasure.

Your tax dollars help support it so why not enjoy an afternoon in one of the many state or national parks across this land?

I like to take a city bus ride. For fifty cents they will take you all over town and you never have to worry about a parking spot.

Sometimes it's difficult to imagine the plight of those less fortunate than us. That's why it is important to volunteer one Saturday to work in a soup kitchen. Compassion comes easy when you see firsthand the needs of others.

Your local high school marching band would love your support at their next contest. You're likely to see talent and dedication that will surprise and delight you.

The next time there is a parade in your town, make plans to go.

●

People collect all kinds of things. Some of them cost a lot of money. But you can have an impressive rock collection just by bending down and picking them up!

●

When the proper time comes, take your daughter or granddaughter on her very first "date." It's a wonderful way to demonstrate how she should expect to be treated now that she is old enough to date. Be sure to take pictures; it will be a very special time for you both!

●

Surely you must know of some field or piece of property that could benefit from you tossing a handful of wildflower seeds on it?

●

There comes a day in everyone's life when you need to throw all your socks away and buy new ones. Today is your day!

Have you ever strolled along in a friend's field and picked some of the wildflowers? They are as beautiful as those you buy and more special because they were grown just for you.

When we want to give Mom a break, the kids and I order pizza from the best parlor in town. Pizza King is a tradition around here, so you might say it's a "traditional" dining treat.

Camping out under the stars is a special treat. You'd be foolish not to use a marble or two for such an adventure.

Everyone should attend a large concert sometime in their life—the larger the better.

Drive around almost any town in the fall and you will likely see a sign for a school festival. Spend a few hours enjoying it. You will likely come home with a pumpkin pie or box of fruit.

have been using my free time for the last year and a half to compile a cookbook based on my mother. She was always in the kitchen—reading cookbooks, eating, or talking about food. I always connect food with her. I inherited a shoebox full of her handwritten recipes and while organizing them I came upon the idea of photocopying them for my brother and sister, and the idea snowballed into a full-scale cookbook. I have included family photos of us gathered together eating, and small stories related to each recipe. The amount of time it will take to complete the project is of no consequence; it's the connection I feel with my mother as I am doing it. I can feel her peering over my shoulder to make sure I am not leaving anything out. The emotion it will bring to my sister and my brother when they see the final product will make it all worthwhile. It is also a way to make sure my children have a true sense of who she was and how much I feel she should have been a large part of their lives.

—Jennifer Alamdari, financial consultant

We love to visit craft shows. The ingenuity that is displayed by these artisans is impressively delightful.

●

It is high time that you write your representatives in government. No matter if you criticize, complain, suggest, admonish, or give them a pat on the back, your contact reaffirms the bond between our government and its people.

●

At least once a year you need to take a moment to read the Declaration of Independence and the Bill of Rights.

●

Someone in your life inspired you to be who you are today. It may have been a parent or other relative, your minister or rabbi, or perhaps a teacher. No matter who it is, you should take time to write them a note to let them know what they meant to you.

Spend an entire Saturday in December in your pajamas.
Rent *Miracle on 34th Street, White Christmas, It's a
Wonderful Life,* and *A Christmas Carol,* and spend the day
watching movies.

●

**Spend the day swimming—not in a pool, in a lake, the
way swimming was intended.**

●

With the lawn carefully groomed, set up the wickets and get
set for a rousing game of croquet.

●

**We've never had a swimming pool. So on those
miserably hot summer days, we set up the hose and
sprinkler in the yard and play. If it's hot enough, even
the dog gets in on the fun.**

●

In almost any town you can find a church fish fry or chili
supper in progress. Buy your tickets and join the fun. These
events aren't haute cuisine but can be places where you
have friends you've yet to meet.

In December you can enjoy a Christmas sing at a local high school or church.

Spend time some Saturday learning a few unique things about the community in which you live. It might make you proud of your hometown and it will give you something interesting to talk about the next time you are with friends.

My wife recently visited a botanical garden in a nearby city. She enjoyed it so much that now we are planning a trip there with the entire family.

Find a recipe for sourdough bread and make it the old-fashioned way—knead the dough by hand. It might turn out just awful, but with practice, you could decide it's a delight.

Share another marble: Volunteer to collect canned food for your community food bank.

On a cool autumn day slowly simmer a Crock-pot of apple cider and cinnamon. The smell is yummy and a hot cup of cider hits the spot!

Plan to attend a symphony in your town or in a nearby city.

You don't have to have children in a local school to enjoy the many plays those young thespians present each year. Tickets are usually inexpensive and the school will appreciate your support.

Until my daughter began to take dance lessons, I never knew how enjoyable a dance recital could be. You don't have to have children to go and enjoy the show.

Surely every town has its own version of a Chat-N-Chew pie shop? Invite your next-door neighbor to join you there for a slice of cherry pie and ice cream.

During a walk around your neighborhood try to collect one of each kind of leaf you can find. People who can identify trees by their leaves always impress me.

Sure, you can buy ice cream at the store, but if you make it yourself you can create your very own flavor and actually know which ingredients were used.

You can't just "go" to the opera. It's an event that must be carefully planned—what you wear, where you eat, and when you arrive. Even so, most people find it well worth the effort.

Building a scale-model boat, plane, or car is an activity that can be enjoyed by nearly everyone. Try it sometime.

You could make a pan of fudge and worry about the calories or you could make a pan of fudge and give half of it to your neighbor. That should appease your conscience and make your neighbor happy too!

Some cool morning you could don your hunting clothes and take to the field in search of deer. When you find them, take careful aim and snap their picture. When the photo is blown up and framed, it will look great over the mantle in your den.

Visit a petting zoo and see the farm animals up close. Take your children, or borrow someone else's for cover!

You can never go wrong watching the movie *Old Yeller* again.

It could make a mess of your kitchen, but making your own taffy isn't a job, it's an adventure!

Treat yourself to a massage from a professional therapist.

Hire a maid for the day.

Start your own indoor herb garden, and when you have friends over for dinner explain how you grew your very own oregano.

•

Launching model rockets may seem like a sport for the young, but I've found that whenever we launch them it attracts a crowd of young and old alike.

•

Some Saturday morning take your doughnuts and thermos of coffee to the local schoolyard and enjoy the soccer game.

•

Make a written list of all your government representatives from town council to governor and from senator to president. Everyone should know who represents him or her.

•

Picking your own blueberries is a fun way to gather the ingredients to make your own ice cream!

A chance to make a mess of your kitchen comes when you make your very own homemade jelly. It's not difficult and besides enjoying it yourself, you'll have plenty to share.

Honey really does come from bees, and the best way to get *really* fresh honey is to visit a local beekeeper. Most of them will show you how it is done if you just ask.

Driving down the highway you'll often see signs to pick your own peaches. Next time you see one, pull off and give it a try.

Visit a farm where you can buy fresh strawberries. It requires a little more effort than buying them in a supermarket, but aren't you worth it?

As a boy, I would walk through the fields with my dad, looking for wild blackberries that often grew along the fencerow. They made the best jellies and pies.

Next Halloween save the pumpkin seeds after carving your jack-o'-lantern. They're delicious roasted and eaten hot right out of the oven.

●

You probably know someone who deplores the walnuts that fall into their yard. You can offer to pick them up and then go to work extracting the tasty nut from the shell.

●

Many people find it enjoyable to take a slow walk through the forest in search of wild mushrooms. You need to learn how to find them but once you know, you too can enjoy this practice.

●

People just don't buy hats like they used to. Although not as common, hats never went out of style. Spend time this Saturday shopping for a new hat.

●

One Saturday afternoon take a helicopter ride and don't forget your camera.

The things I do to relax tend to be very strenuous.
I can't understand it. I do love to fly helicopters.
That's the best combination of adrenaline and
serenity I have found so far.

—Gary Chapman,
country music singer

Years ago some folks enjoyed playing chess by mail with a distant partner. The game could take months or years to complete. These days e-mail or electronic chess makes it easier but it's still fun. Find a long-distance partner and give it a try.

*

Small airports almost always offer a low-cost ride in good weather. On a clear Saturday afternoon make a visit and see if you can take a ride in a small plane. It's nothing like flying on a major airline!

*

I like to attend the annual hog roast sponsored by the volunteer fire department. Almost all our neighbors attend so it is another chance to spend time getting to know them.

*

Spend the afternoon at a nearby horse track.

When was the last time you climbed a tree? Nothing will take you back to your youth like climbing a tree— skinned knees and all.

On a lazy summer day, we like to ride our bicycles to the nearby elementary school. The kids enjoy the playground while we relax under a shady tree.

Carefully picking out your Christmas tree and then getting it safely home is a family event that usually takes an entire afternoon. There are bonus points for buying a tree in the snow!

Spend the day decorating your Christmas tree. Don't forget the strings of popcorn and cranberries.

Where can you learn about farm life, watch a demolition derby and a high school band contest, ride a tilt-a-whirl until you are sick, and then top it off with cotton candy? The county fair, of course!

Throughout the Christmas season in Cincinnati, the local power company sets up a big model train exhibit for all to see. It's a wonderful tradition that is worth visiting each year.

●

There is probably no better way to cool off on a hot summer day than with a lazy inner-tube ride down the river.

●

Spend time to research and document your family tree. It's information that many families don't have but all would like.

●

Visit a craftsman fair and peruse the handiwork talent on display.

●

Enroll your dog in obedience school and spend the time required with your pet to make it a good pet citizen.

●

Spend the morning visiting an Amish community to see how some people live their lives without the benefit of modern technology.

No matter where you live there are always free concerts for you to attend. Sometimes the talent is good and sometimes it is poor, but either way you get what you paid for!

•

At least once a year you should invite your pastor out for a round of golf (yes, you should pay).

•

Send a bouquet of flowers to someone you work with who does an exemplary job but rarely gets the credit he deserves.

•

This Saturday, determine that you will leave your car parked and either walk, ride a bicycle, or use public transportation wherever you go.

•

I like to hit a bucket of golf balls at a heated driving range on a cold winter day.

When the winds of winter howl it's a good time to stay indoors and curl up with a good book and a hot cup of tea.

•

Treat yourself or your wife to a full day at the beauty salon or spa—we're talking the hair, a facial, manicure, pedicure, the works!

•

At least once in your life you need to bring a bottle of Dom Pérignon and fresh strawberries to your sleeping wife.

•

Owning and maintaining a home is a lifelong venture. Each room is a special project. Make plans and begin remodeling one room at a time.

•

Restoring an old chair or other piece of furniture is like breathing new life into an old friend. Be patient and don't hurry. It doesn't have to be done in one day.

Every year I promise myself that I will take the time to write a personal note to include with each Christmas card we send. And each year we barely have time to get just the cards out. This year, make it a point to spend an afternoon writing personal notes to include with your cards.

●

Share another marble and help your heart out too. Volunteer to raise money for a good cause by walking in a walkathon.

●

No matter where you live, your local hospital would love for you to volunteer to work there for a day.

●

Spend the afternoon taking your very fondest family photo to an artist and find out what it would cost to make an oil painting of it. You'll cherish it for life.

●

A trip to the park with a bag of popcorn to feed the ducks is a pretty good use of a marble if you ask me.

A progressive dinner with a lot of friends can be a great way to add unwanted pounds! Have appetizers at one place, then everyone moves to the next home for the main course, followed by dessert at yet another home.

A shopping trip to a large farmer's market can be great fun, and it is somehow satisfying to buy garden fresh vegetables instead of "freezer filler."

Every now and then I think that you should get dressed up and have dinner at one of those fancy restaurants that slowly revolves, providing a spectacular view of the city.

My wife calls it a "cheap date" when I take her to a half-priced Saturday matinee and make a fast-food stop afterward. But she never declines to go along!

Find a World War II veteran and have him tell you about his part in the war. Very soon they will all be gone and all we'll have is a secondhand account of that terrible time.

●

No matter what your taste, somebody, somewhere is playing or singing the music you love. Find them and enjoy it!

●

When was the last time you attended a play or other live dramatic performance? Search your paper for a schedule and enjoy one this Saturday.

●

At least once a year we like to visit the state capital building. Such a trip is always an educational adventure for all of us and the kids love to go.

●

Next time you take a walk in a city park and you come across an old statue of some fellow you've never heard of, write down his name and do a little research to discover who he is and why he merited such favor.

A trip to a large museum is time well spent. Everyone learns something and it always makes me thankful that I don't live in "the good old days."

●

Buy a foreign language CD and some rainy Saturday morning learn to say, "Hello, it is nice to meet you" and "Which way is the rest room?" in another tongue.

●

Look for a church bake sale to attend. You'll probably get a good deal on a cake or pie and you might be pleasantly surprised by who you meet.

●

There is a place in our town where model hobbyists fly their radio-controlled airplanes. On a crisp, clear Saturday morning I like to show up there with coffee and bagels and watch them fly.

●

Learning how to build and fly them myself would be another challenge altogether, and a great way to spend a few weekends with my son or daughter.

One Saturday morning in October we like to visit a large farm that sells pumpkins. Several small ones make nice autumn decorations, but the *big* one is going to become our jack-o'-lantern.

•

Winter is not so bad. Football, basketball, hockey—need I go on?

•

I've found that some of the best conversations I've ever had take place while pitching horseshoes with a friend or relative on a Saturday afternoon.

•

A five-thousand-piece jigsaw puzzle is a challenge made for a rainy Saturday afternoon.

•

Putting colors on canvas can be a lot of fun, and you don't have to be an artist to enjoy it. Try it early in the morning to catch the best light.

Spend time searching for long-lost relatives online. It seems that nearly everyone has e-mail these days.

•

Ivanhoe's has the best ice cream and sundaes in the state. Despite the twelve-mile ride to get there, we never have to say "let's go" to the kids more than once!

•

Our Labrador loves it when we take him to the river. He is always the first one in the water and the last one out. We can spend the entire afternoon playing with the dog.

•

A friendly game of touch football in the backyard is always a big hit with the kids and their friends.

•

Pete's Grocery is a little country store a few miles from our house. Pete keeps a comfortable bench in a shady spot out in front of the store. We like to ride our bicycles there, buy a soda pop, and enjoy the shady rest before making the ride back home.

Have you ever ridden a horse? There is a park near here where you can pay a few dollars and ride a horse through the park. I've never met a soul who didn't enjoy doing that!

My daughter loves it when we stay out in the yard late and catch lightning bugs. They glow in the jar where we keep them, but Jamie *insists* that we turn them loose before the night is over.

I like to go to the state fair. The rides, the farm animals, and the demolition derby along with corndogs, elephant ears, and cotton candy make for a great time.

Sometimes I've found it worthwhile to borrow something that I don't really need. It gives me a good excuse to spend time with the person I borrowed it from twice—when I borrow it, and when I return it.

Take your family for a large breakfast, but do it early enough in the morning so there is no waiting for a table.

*

Invite a group over for a euchre tournament. Just make sure your spouse is not your partner.

*

Mow the grass, trim the hedge, pull the weeds, and enjoy it. It isn't a chore; think of it as "yard art" and you are the artisan making it what you will.

*

You don't have to be a great handyman to buy an old cabinet and restore it. You do have to be a great human being to then give it as a gift to someone you care about.

*

Spend some time on your rooftop and you'll come away with a fresh perspective of your neighborhood. You'll probably also find something that needs fixing up there!

A backyard barbecue including your neighbors and their kids is a great way to spend a Saturday afternoon.

Have you ever ridden a train? Around here you can take an enjoyable two-hour train ride and it is well worth the effort.

I once spent nearly an entire Saturday trying to explain to my son why there is snow on mountaintops despite the fact that hot air rises. I don't recommend it!

A daylong trip to an amusement park will make you a hero with your kids, at least for a day.

We like to visit a neighborhood rummage sale on Saturday morning. It is a *great* affirmation that our neighbors have as much (or more) junk as we do.

A wise father will find a way to get his wife and kids to help wash and wax the car on a Saturday morning (please write me when you figure out how to do this).

•

Once a year my dad spends a day cleaning up around the grave markers of all our relatives. It isn't a fun job but one that needs doing, and one that I will assume someday. It's a good way to connect with my roots and learn a little more about my family.

•

Our Labrador retriever gets a bath once a month. Have I mentioned that Sammy doesn't care much for those Saturdays?

•

You are never too old for a long barefoot walk in the grass or on a sandy beach. Make the time and try it.

•

The job of raking leaves is a lot less of a chore when we pile them up and jump in them with the kids.

You don't have to go camping to enjoy roasting marshmallows. My son and his girlfriend started a fire in the backyard and enjoyed them right there. They even let my wife join in on the festivities!

Here in Indiana we still have covered bridge festivals (remember *The Bridges of Madison County*?). We went to one last year and I bought a 1959 auto license plate that I hung up in my garage.

Brenda convinced me to take her to a boat and travel show one Saturday despite my protests. As it turned out, we had a *great* time and look forward to doing it again.

Family Fun Day at our house means the day in the park with the kids, dog, some sandwiches, the Frisbee, and a football.

I like to take long, solitary walks in the woods very early in the morning.

There's a restaurant here in town where people with vintage automobiles tend to congregate on Saturday nights. It is a lot of fun to walk around looking at the old cars and talking to those who proudly restore them.

Attending a Saturday-night high school basketball game here in Indiana is not only required, but also a good way to see seven thousand other rabid fans, friends, and neighbors in action!

At least once a year you have to load up the family and attend a major league ball game—even if you have to drive a hundred miles or so.

Find a park near a lake and enjoy a picnic there, taking a walk around the lake when you are finished.

Tell your kids a story about a relative or friend whom you haven't spoken with in ages. Then call him or her and say, "I was just talking about you. . . ."

Watch the Saturday-morning cartoons with your children.

*

Rent the video *Casablanca* and watch it, noting that Bogey *never* actually says, "Play it again, Sam."

*

Take a tour of a historic house or building in your area.

*

Load the family into the car and take a drive into the country. It's *always* better if you *try* to get lost on such a trip!

*

Plan to spend a few hours rummaging through a local flea market. Don't leave until you've spent at least two hours there.

*

I like to visit old cemeteries and read the inscriptions on the oldest grave markers.

*

Take a bike ride to a place you've never been before.

Go fishing. Remember, a bad day of fishing beats a good day of working anytime.

●

I like to take the family to the shopping mall. They like to shop but I enjoy just watching all the people.

●

Have you ever taken a ride in a hot air balloon? Neither have I, but I plan to spend a marble doing just that one day.

●

On a warm summer day, I like to spread a blanket on the ground and take a nap. There is nothing like sleeping outside.

●

Spend the morning at a fancy bookstore—the kind with a coffee shop. Buy a cup and browse the new books. Sure, it's four dollars a cup, but it's *latte!*

●

Some Saturdays we all agree to *not* turn on the television for the entire day. The quiet in the house is worth a marble.

Take a long walk. It's even better if you go so far that you have to stop for dinner before returning home.

I like to search on the Internet for people who went to Muncie Central High School when I did.

On occasion, I've actually cooked something new from the recipe on the side of the macaroni and cheese box. You should try it!

Flying a kite is a wonderful way to spend a lazy Saturday afternoon.

When the kids were young they used to like it when we would park near the end of the runway at the airport and watch the planes take off and land. I still like to do that.

Take a homemade cake or muffins to an elderly or shut-in neighbor.

Next time, make it an entire meal. And bring enough for yourself, too, so you can enjoy his or her company. You'll both be glad you did.

Notes are rarely handwritten anymore. That makes them special. Send a handwritten note to someone today.

Surprise your parents with a box of decadent doughnuts and an early Saturday-morning visit.

Spend the day planning your next vacation. Get the road atlas and travel brochures out for everyone to see. The anticipation can be as good as the trip.

Tell your children a true story about a time when you got into trouble when you were their age.

Spend the entire day in your pajamas reading *Raise the Titanic* by Clive Cussler.

My bath is my sanctuary. It's the place where I can wash off all the stuff of the day. I soak in a hot tub and put on a nice pair of pajamas.

—Oprah Winfrey

Do the grocery shopping one Saturday with your spouse.

Visit an old farm auction and marvel at the antique furniture.

Visit your local library and spend an hour reading the newspaper from the largest city that they have.

Volunteer to work a few hours at your local animal shelter. Go ahead, let yourself fall in love with a puppy.

Do some research and locate a teacher you had in school. Send him or her a thank-you card for having done such a good job.

Stop by your church or synagogue and ask if you can help clean up the inside or work in the yard.

People love exotic animals. A family trip to the zoo will make a lifetime of memories. Bring your camera.

*

Spend one Saturday morning organizing all your old photos. Use the opportunity to share stories about your relatives and early life with your children.

*

Make an impressive breakfast, complete with a single flower, and serve your spouse breakfast in bed.

*

Rent several of your favorite movies the night before and have an all-day "film fest" on Saturday.

*

I like to listen to *A Prairie Home Companion* on National Public Radio every Saturday night.

*

Order a dozen long-stemmed roses for your mother-in-law. On the card, thank her for your spouse.

Many years ago when my business first began having problems I started taking Wednesday nights off and going to O'Dowds, a local bar. No matter what was going on I went. Weather didn't matter, time of year, holidays, guests in town. There was no excuse that would keep me away. I even planned my business trips so that I left on Thursdays and returned on Wednesday mornings. I didn't always feel like going, but I went anyway, knowing that after a while I would be glad I was there. I am not saying there were never any bad nights, but they were few and far between.

My mother and I shared the e-mail version of "A Thousand Marbles" shortly before she was diagnosed with cancer. On the day she was given ninety days to live she counted out marbles at my house. She said, "Remember that story about the marbles? That's my ninety days." Her hands cupped as she scooped them off the bed. It was very difficult for her to get them all in her hands, yet she did not stop till she was able to squeeze or stack every one, as if to leave one behind would be giving up a day. It was quite profound to hold the rest of your life in your hands.

The day my mother died, exactly ninety days later, I went to her house in search of some last bit of wisdom she may have written down before it was too late. There was a lot there; she was quite prolific in those final days. But in the drawer of her desk were her ninety marbles. It was Wednesday. I was carrying marbles in my pocket that night when I went to O'Dowds.

After four years, I have an unending supply of stories about Wednesdays at O'Dowds. But they all have the same moral. If you don't take time for yourself now, you are going to run out.

—Mike Sager, entrepreneur

Your brother-in-law will sure be surprised when you show up early one morning with a box of new batteries to replace those in his smoke detectors. And don't forget the doughnuts.

Order Thai food to go and invite your closest friends over for a late-night dinner and a movie.

We enjoy viewing the night sky and the kids compete to see who can see the most falling stars on a given night.

Show your wife and kids how to change a tire on the car.

Read one chapter of the book *A Wrinkle in Time* to your children each Saturday until it's complete.

Make a trip into the attic—determined to throw something away!

At least once a year you should go to a new car dealer and let them show you all the new models. Take a test drive. Enjoy their coffee and doughnuts. You don't have to buy a thing.

I love to visit an apple orchard in September. Fresh apples, cider, apple pies, apple butter . . .

Take the kids to Grandma's house and enjoy a romantic, candlelit dinner with your spouse at home.

I enjoy a lazy canoe ride down the White River on a Saturday afternoon.

Set your alarm for 4:30 A.M. When you awake, take a fresh cup of coffee out in the backyard and wait and watch the sunrise.

Visit that vegetable stand alongside the road and enjoy a chat with the owner while you are picking out the freshest tomatoes.

●

Visit a lake and walk along the shore skipping rocks across the water.

●

Snuggle up on the couch with a warm comforter and the television remote control so you don't have to get up for hours.

●

Don't miss the chance to have your voice heard: Register to vote!

●

Take turns making it a "special" day for one of your children. She picks the movie to watch, what's for dinner, and what to have for dessert.

Running around the yard catching snowflakes on your tongue might be silly, but you won't know that it is until you give it a try.

You'll never know just how fast a 90-mph fastball is until you visit one of those places where they measure your pitching speed.

Find an old mantle clock and have it repaired. The sounds of it ticking and sounding on the hour will warm your home.

Learn your state bird, state flower, and state song. Only about 5 percent of people know those things about their own state. Welcome to an elite group!

Turn all the power off one evening—lights, television, heating, and air. Spend your powerless evening quietly conversing in the glow of a candle.

Spend the day repotting your houseplants or working in your flower bed. There is something therapeutic about having your hands in the dirt.

Remember the fun you had as a kid rolling down a snow-covered hill? I dare you to do it again!

For the less rambunctious but still adventuresome: Slide down a snowy hill on a piece of cardboard.

Hot chocolate with whipped cream topping is a wonderful accompaniment to warming up by the fireplace.

Take a good book with you and read it while relaxing alongside a lazy river.

Is there anything more relaxing than rocking in a chair on the front porch during a warm summertime rain?

Make small talk with a senior citizen today. You'll make them feel special and it's likely that you'll learn something.

•

Take off your shoes and socks and sit on a pier with your feet dangling in the water.

•

I like to look through old photos on a rainy day with a hot cup of flavored coffee.

•

A bowl of cookies-and-cream ice cream and two spoons will make you a very popular person for a short time!

•

Take a ride on a snowmobile and enjoy the heavy snowfall. It's funny how you seldom get cold while riding in the snow.

•

On this trip to the beach, rent a pair of Jet Skis and fly across the water with the spray in your face.

Next time you bring a video home to watch make a big batch of buttery popccrn, turn off the lights, and enjoy the show. You just saved twenty dollars!

Relax tonight and enjoy a sumptuous frozen dinner. Make it your goal to have no dishes to wash when you are done.

Spend the morning playing in the park with your dog. He could use the exercise and so could you!

Make a list of every teacher you can recall from a school you attended. Then call your best friend who went to that school with you and see how many teachers he can remember.

Save a few crossword puzzles from the newspaper. Some quiet morning when you are the first to rise, dig into them with a steaming cup of Earl Grey tea.

Rent an Elvis Presley movie and sing along with the King.

•

Locate an amateur ("ham") radio operator and have her tell you all about the hobby.

•

Send a handwritten note or card to a friend who is feeling down.

•

When those Girl Scout cookies you ordered finally show up, take them to your aunt's house for a visit.

•

Let your voice be heard. Join a community singing group.

•

Have pancakes, bacon, and eggs for dinner tonight. Breakfast for dinner is a nice change of pace for you, and a lot of fun for the kids.

Write a story just for yourself. No one else has to see it and it will give you a project to work on.

•

I like to watch the old *Victory at Sea* videos when I'm stuck inside on a bad weather day.

•

At some point you must round up all those pennies you've been collecting in jars, cups, and bottles and take them to the bank.

•

Or, for fun, dump them all on the floor instead. Gather all your kids to count and roll them up before you take them to the bank. Your teller will thank you!

•

If you're like me you have a computer. But I still have important phone numbers, Christmas card lists, addresses, passwords, and all kinds of personal information scribbled on notebooks, cards, and Post-it notes. Someday I am going to record all that data in a database on my computer. You should too!

Do you have any idea of the joy you could bring a soon-to-drive niece or nephew when you pick them up one Saturday morning, take them to a shopping mall parking lot, and have them practice parking your car?

*

Buy yourself a new deck of cards so that you can enjoy a cup of coffee and a game of solitaire while the snow is falling outside.

*

Everybody has one: It's that thing in your garage that you have no idea what it is, how it got there, or why you've kept it for this long. *Today* is the day to put an ad in the newspaper to sell it.

*

Let the kids make a batch of ice pops on a hot summer day.

*

Spend a few hours playing video games on the PlayStation with your kids. They'll enjoy the time you spend with them and you'll find out what kind of games they play.

Volunteer to help out at your church car wash. If they don't have one, why not organize it for them?

Swing on a rope over water and jump in!

Make boats out of paper with your kids and see whose stays afloat the longest.

Take a jar to a pond or creek one afternoon and try to catch a tadpole.

Brew a large pitcher of tea in the sunlight, and when it's done, add a load of ice and share it with your neighbor.

Buy your very own box of sixty-four crayons—the kind with the sharpener on the back. You'd be surprised how much fun you'll have coloring at any age.

With everyone out of the house and doing their own thing, put the musical *Oklahoma* in the VCR and sing along as loud as you like.

Hang peaceful-sounding wind chimes outside your bedroom window and let them put you to sleep.

Decorate a tree in your yard with festive lights even when it isn't Christmas.

Have everything you need on hand so you and the kids can make your very own tie-dye T-shirts one day. So what if you only wear them on weekends when you're sure you won't see anybody else. You've had a lot of fun making them!

There is a creek near my house and at one place alongside the creek there is a large rock. I like to sit on that rock and enjoy the view. My kids call that my "thinking" rock. Everyone should have a place like that. Do you?

I like it when my daughter climbs on my lap and falls asleep in my arms.

•

Take old rings, earrings, and necklaces to the jeweler's to have them redesigned into a new piece.

•

Buy a mother's ring as a gift for your mother-in-law.

•

Give your kitchen a makeover on the cheap. Put up a new border around the kitchen today.

•

Every real kitchen has a cookie jar. Make sure you shop carefully for the perfect cookie jar for yours. The children and grandchildren will remember that jar for a lifetime.

•

Take time today to order printed return address stickers. It's so nice when you pay bills or send cards to not have to write your address over and over.

Create a job jar so those "honey-do" tasks can be added with the agreement that you will draw at least one task out a week.

•

Spend an afternoon at the roller-skating rink and stop for ice cream on the way home.

•

Plan a nice dinner and enjoy it outside on the patio.

•

Go ahead and list all of your New Year's resolutions for next year so you can get a head start on breaking them!

•

Bring out your creative side and make a video- or audiotape to send to a distant relative.

•

Enjoy a hot bowl of oatmeal for breakfast this morning and take as much time reading the newspaper as you like. Don't forget the comics!

In the helter-skelter push and pull of Senate life, Hadassah and I have found that our religious observances provide very welcome relief, particularly the Sabbath. . . . It is a day apart when my family and I are able to reconnect with one another and with our spiritual selves, to pray, to talk, to read, to rest or just to plain enjoy ourselves. . . . In fact, I usually don't wear a watch on the Sabbath. I treasure that time, twenty-four hours of no meetings, no telephone calls, no television, no radio, no traveling, no business of any sort.

—Joseph Lieberman, U.S. senator

Take a frosty early-morning walk with your dog. If you are out for at least an hour you've earned a morning nap.

•

Our kids like it when we turn the television sound down during a ball game and lip-sync the play-by-play action ourselves. Don't knock it until you've tried it!

•

A few hours playing on a trampoline could quite possibly add marbles to your jar.

•

Take your dog with you to the doughnut shop this morning and don't forget to get him a cream-filled.

•

Gather all of the shoes in your house that need shining and go to work on them like a seasoned shoe shiner. Since your hands are going to get messy, you might even volunteer to shine shoes of the old man next door while you're at it.

Making your own homemade noodles is the best excuse I know for buying one of those fancy pasta makers for the kitchen.

Give up the bean and make today a No Caffeine Day. If you find yourself suffering with an unbearable headache you may be a java junkie!

A wood board propped up on a block makes an ideal jump ramp for a bicycle or skateboard. The kids will think you are *très* cool.

Spend the evening telling made-up stories to each other while sitting in the dark.

Enjoy a lazy afternoon nap in front of a toasty fireplace.

Break in your new snow blower by clearing first your driveway and then your neighbor's after a big snowfall.

Take stock of your life by writing down on paper everything that you have to be grateful for. I think the length of your list will pleasantly surprise you.

Nephews, nieces, grandchildren, and children will all appreciate your thoughtfulness when you see something about them in the newspaper and you clip the article and put it in a frame to present to them next time you see them.

Everyone needs a will. If you don't have one, then spend a marble and have one made up today.

Sometimes I like to go to lunch by myself. When I do, I stop by the bookstore and pick up a magazine to enjoy while having lunch. Solitude can be refreshing.

Spend the day with the oldest relative that you can and record the event on video- or audiotape. Fifteen years from now you'll be glad that you did.

Once we paid an artist to make cartoon caricatures of the kids. We photocopied the artwork and had them framed. These continue to be treasured on the grandparents' wall.

●

The next time you wash your own car offer to wash an elderly neighbor's car as well. It could begin a trend in your neighborhood.

●

You'll be a welcomed guest when you show up at your in-laws' one Saturday morning with a warm basket of fresh-baked muffins.

●

Hire a limousine to take your parents out to dinner on their next birthday.

●

Standing in your backyard or at a park, take a few shots kicking a football as far as you possibly can. You can work off a lot of frustration by pounding the pigskin and then chasing it down.

Make an effort to get to know your butcher on a first-name basis and the steaks you prepare will become the things legends are made of.

Volunteer to coach a Little League or intramural team in your community. The kids need someone to look up to and you could be it!

Today is a great day to send your spouse a bouquet of flowers.

Get a look at the new models before they hit the showroom by attending a car show.

This holiday season set aside one day to take an elderly neighbor or relative who is no longer mobile shopping with you. It takes a special kind of person to help care for the aged and we could certainly use a lot more who do.

Almost everyone listens to talk radio at some time or another. Go ahead and call them up and give them a piece of your mind. You'll feel better after you do.

It isn't safe to turn the young ones loose with fireworks. This year for Independence Day plan a backyard party for the kids where you can have a blast (literally) while you oversee the smoke bombs, fountains, and sparklers.

Spend a sweaty morning at the gym learning to use all that modern equipment that was designed especially to make you hurt.

Today would be a good time to open a new savings account—one exclusively to save money for that once-in-a-lifetime vacation that you will soon take.

Indulge yourself a bit and have your shirts monogrammed today. It's a classy touch and one that you won't regret.

When was the last time you wrote a love letter? Isn't it about time that you took an hour and told someone just how much you love her?

Go to a men's store and be fitted for a new suit today. You don't have to wait for a funeral to buy a new suit!

In the dark of evening, after a thunderstorm, search the yard with a flashlight for night crawlers. It's cheap fishing bait—and the mysterious goings-on in your yard will give your neighbors something to talk about!

Carefully peel the skin from an apple in a single, continuous long piece!

Order an American flag that has hung over the nation's capitol from your senator's office and then give it as a special gift to a veteran in your family.

After a summer thunderstorm, take the kids out to splash in the puddles in your yard. It's especially fun for them after a hailstorm, because of the mysteriously large chunks of ice in the yard. Yes, you may have to repair damage to your lawn later on, but your children will remember it for the rest of their lives!

Make time to pray today. Most people find that prayer really does change things.

Make a visit to one of your old schools. You'll be amazed how the old place looks after so many years.

A cookie sheet full of shelled peanuts makes a delicious aroma roasting in your oven.

Did you go to summer camp when you were young? Volunteer to be a camp counselor or teach a camp class next summer. It will revive a treasure chest full of youthful memories.

Spend an hour remembering your high school hijinks while browsing through your old yearbook. Do it with your children to give them a good laugh and a new insight into their very uncool parents.

•

Open up and enjoy an icy cold bottle of soda pop. It doesn't count unless it is in a glass bottle and so cold it is nearly frozen.

•

The next time you are driving in the country and pass a field of cows, go ahead and roll down the window and "moo" loudly at them. You know you want to.

•

Play a game of kick-the-can down a neighborhood street that doesn't see much traffic.

•

Fill the largest trough or bucket you can find with water and toss in a dozen apples and declare that the annual family apple bobbing has begun!

Spend a little time remembering what your very favorite songs were when you were in high school. Track them down, make a recording, and play it for your children or grandchildren. They may laugh when they hear it, but you will all have a great time.

●

Organize a neighborhood block party!

●

On a glorious summer day go to the drive-in food stand and have a Coney dog and root beer in your front seat.

●

Load up the car and find a drive-in movie theater. There aren't many left to enjoy, so you'd better hurry!

●

Take an old comfortable pair of shoes to a repair shop instead of throwing them out. It's not often that you can replace a sole for a sawbuck.

●

Take a romantic ride with someone you love on a bicycle built for two.

Go for a refreshing skinny dip on a moonless night!

◦

Feeling mischievous? Carve your initials on a tree in the woods.

◦

If you take a board and checkers to a retirement home, you won't have to look hard for someone to play a few games with.

◦

After the harvest take a walk through a cornfield and pick up some fallen ears. They make good food for the squirrels when the snow has covered the ground.

◦

If you live in the countryside, you probably have older neighbors with generous gardens. Offer to help them harvest their vegetables now and again. They'll likely send you home with enough produce to last at least a week!

On a nice fall day, once the nuts really start to fall, take some family or friends to a country road or grove where the pecan trees grow, and pick your own pecans. Warning: Teenagers tend to think of this as a chore, but you'll need at least one to climb the trees and shake the stubborn nuts loose from the limbs!

Share a little of yourself with someone who could use a friend. Volunteer to be a Big Brother or Big Sister.

Take a short vacation and finally visit that friend who moved across the country.

Have an old-fashioned wiener roast. Make a clearing, gather fallen and pruned tree branches, and bring your neighbors together for hot dogs and smores on a cool autumn night.

Lie in the snow and make "angels."

Play a family game of Name That Tune by humming or whistling the theme songs for television shows. Find out who is the champ in your crew.

·

Take a long walk on a winding country road.

·

On a cold rainy day when you just can't seem to get warm, take the longest hot shower in history. Follow it up with a warm robe and socks fresh from the dryer.

·

Buy a smoker and smoke your very own ham or turkey. You might decide it's the only way to cook!

·

Lie on your bed, stare at the ceiling, and let your mind wander. Once life speeds up, we are rarely alone and are often too "busy" to spend precious solitary moments just thinking. But those moments can be productive and healing, and they can let your soul take a deep breath and your shoulders shrug off some of the weight that's always on them.

Dress up on Halloween and go out with friends to a sit-down dinner at your favorite "haunt."

*

It's never too late to try your hand at expressing yourself on canvas! Many famous artists started late in life, and even if you don't become famous, you'll have something your family will treasure forever.

*

Go with friends on an inexpensive close-to-home trip and absorb the sights of a nearby town.

*

Write a book. Who cares if it ever gets published?

*

Take your children, nieces, or nephews to a pond with plenty of rocks and teach them to skip rocks, or have a "biggest splash" contest.

*

Head to the woods before dawn on a crisp spring morning and sit still as you listen to the woods wake up.

Build a "fort" or "clubhouse" with the kids out of lawn chairs and old blankets.

If you live near a hay field, you know there's usually a good long delay between making the hay bales and taking them away for the animals. Get permission if you need to, but take the kids one afternoon to play on them. Remember not to destroy any, or you'll never be invited back.

If you live in the city, try not to take it for granted. Use the parks, see the shows, patronize the museums. For heaven's sake, there are people out there playing on hay bales!

Teach your ten-year-old daughter how to play gin rummy. Have a plate full of Archway apple cookies on the side.

On a sunny warm day take your kids for a drive. Roll down the windows, turn up the radio, and sing along real loud.

Next time there is a comet or meteor shower, invite friends over at midnight, dust off the telescope, and have a cosmos-viewing party.

Go for a drive in the country on a spring day and look for young animals frolicking in the fields.

Go to a tall, popular tourist attraction like the Empire State Building or St. Louis Arch and climb to the very top. It's okay to take the elevator.

Pick up a harmonica and play a tune—or whatever sound comes out!

Check out a local community theater production. Some of these companies are actually quite good, and you can be sure that everyone involved, from the actors to the box office manager, have worked very hard to put on a great show. (Most people involved in community theater work day jobs, too!) Ticket prices are usually very reasonable.

This December, find out if any community theaters or high schools are performing *A Christmas Carol*. This age-old story is even more heartwarming when experienced in person.

•

Call the community theaters in your area and ask whether you and your family can volunteer. Most will welcome the help—you might be asked to build or paint sets, hang lights (for adults and older kids), sew costumes, or sell tickets. Rather than seeming like work, it's actually a lot of fun to contribute to a great show!

•

Call around to your area's professional theaters and ask whether they have a volunteer usher program. Usually you just have to show up one or more hours before show time, tear tickets, stick around during intermission, and you can see the show for free!

Before the days of television, radio, and movies, people entertained one another at gatherings. Host a potluck dinner for family and friends. Each family should bring a dish, and each guest (and hosting family members) must prepare a "piece": recite a favorite poem, sing a song, play a musical instrument, or perform a short sketch. It doesn't have to be perfectly polished, and bonus points can be given for inviting audience participation!

If you are planning to redecorate or renovate your house, have a special prepainting party. Your kids and their friends can draw or paint on the walls as much as they please—just this once. When else would they get free license to do that? The only rules: *walls only,* and no crayons or other waxy or oily materials (they're difficult to paint over).

Turn off the TV. Get out of the house. Walk.

Take a noncredit, continuing education class from a local college and learn something new.

On a Saturday morning one winter, I got up early and my husband stayed in bed. I was going to work on my computer while he slept, but when I looked out and saw about six inches of snow, I woke him up and told him. He got so excited and wanted to go out immediately—he'd had a sled for five years that he hadn't ever got to use. So out we went, and our five-year-old neighbor came over and they spent about an hour sliding down and coming back up our driveway, which is very steep!

They had a ball and I took many pictures. Our neighbor, Zach, had never seen a sled, but he was very familiar with four-wheelers. His comment was, "This is such fun, more fun than vacation . . . this is two thumbs up!"

—Teressa McGary, wife and mother

Take a car ride instead of watching TV—while you're out, indulge in an ice cream treat or a slushie.

•

Hang a birdfeeder outside your window, and enjoy the variety of birds that visit.

•

Take a moment of time to give thanks for what's good in your life instead of dwelling on the bad.

•

Buy a dog or adopt one from your local shelter. It will reward you with unconditional love.

•

Buy a small, manageable counted cross-stitch or needlework project and finish it. Needlework is very relaxing, and you will have a wonderful sense of accomplishment when you see your handiwork.

•

Spend an afternoon browsing through a used-book store.

Buy a large puzzle, a thousand pieces or more, and work on
it a little every evening as a family. Puzzle working builds
family camaraderie as everyone can contribute a small part
for the larger whole.

**Steer clear of the malls and patronize the small
neighborhood shops you have seen but never visited
before.**

Pick out your Christmas tree from a real tree farm,
preferably one that includes a horse-driven sleigh ride.

**Visit a paint-your-own-pottery shop and create an
original piece of art.**

Go to a high school football or basketball game, even if you
don't have any connection to the school. Root for the home
team.

When I'm on the road, the band and I carry several bikes in the luggage bay of the bus, and I'm out riding nearly every day. Most cities have great paths along rivers or botanical gardens to ride around. We also hit museums and cool places of interest in the area in the few hours we have before sound check. Those things help you keep it together on a lot of levels.

**—Bonnie Raitt,
singer and songwriter**

Go to book signings sponsored by your local independent bookstore, even if you have never heard of the author.

•

Visit a church different from the one that you are most familiar with.

•

Participate in a charity run or walk event. You don't have to be a runner to enjoy it.

•

Spend a day going to the tourist attractions in your town that you have never visited.

•

Enroll in a foreign language class for the language of a country you have always wanted to visit.

•

Ask your aunt or grandmother to teach you to knit or crochet.

It doesn't have to be a dark and stormy night for you to build a fire and play Monopoly.

Kiss someone you love in the rain.

Where are you? Stand still for thirty seconds and listen to all the sounds, smell all the smells, and *really* take note of everything around you. Now try it somewhere else and notice the differences.

Take pictures of your family wherever you are. Any time spent with them is memorable.

Take a walk when it's snowing and enjoy the silence of the snow falling.

Enjoy the outdoors—wander the forests, hunt, fish, climb mountains, run rivers, breathe deeply, and appreciate the fresh air.

Play with your dog or your kids. Reserve at least an hour of time for it, and don't take any calls!

•

Sing as loud as you can to your favorite song even if you don't have a good voice.

•

Smile at small children. Make them laugh if you can!

•

Plan a small surprise for someone you know at least once a month.

•

On a day when no one else is home, close the curtains, put on your favorite music, and *dance!*

•

On cold Saturday mornings I build a fire in the fireplace, pour a cup of coffee, and read the paper in my pajamas. On warm Saturday mornings, I take my paper and coffee outside and read on the deck under the sun umbrella.

Every once in a while, try to experience life from the perspective of a toddler. They are awed by so many things we overlook in our everyday lives. Delight in the houses decorated with pretty lights at Christmas, the wonder of a train, the beauty of fireworks, the things that amazed us when you were a child, the things you should take the time to enjoy again.

Institute a family game night. Enjoy an assortment of board games, munchies, and music. Remember to turn off the TV.

Let the kids cook or order dinner to go that night.

Take time to teach your children to love and respect nature.

Spend five solid minutes in the evening petting your dog. Your dog will love it, and you will feel peaceful and serene.

Build something. Anything. My husband and I recently built a brick patio, and even though it took several weekends for us to do, we had the greatest feeling of accomplishment when we were done. Every day we look out and see it and remark that it is the most beautiful patio we have ever seen. We don't see the crooked bricks, or the area where the spacing got off and we had to do some creative brickwork. We feel good about it and can't wait until summer when we can spend many marbles sitting outside, enjoying it. Next spring I plan on building a potting bench—another marble.

*

I loved looking through the Sunday ads with my family over breakfast. More so around Christmas, when we would make our wish list from the ads as well as make our to-buy list before we went shopping.

*

Go for a long motorcycle ride.

*

Become a volunteer for a cause you are passionate about.

Try your hand at an "extreme" sport such as white-water rafting or snowboarding. It's exhilarating, and learning a new skill is always satisfying.

Bake chocolate chip cookies from scratch on a rainy day.

Take your dog for long, leisurely walks at your favorite park. It's good for both of you.

Plan the vacation of your dreams, then dig in and take it whether you can afford it or not.

For holiday surprises have an in-house scavenger hunt for your kids. They get a note giving a clue to the next note and so on until they find their surprise gift at the end.

My kids delighted in Saturday-morning pancakes. The special treat while waiting for them was to be served "mini" pancakes that I made while the big ones finished cooking.

For children in first and second grades, add a note to their lunch sacks each day. On the note put: Today is [day, month, date, year]. Add a little smiley face and "I love you" to it! It will help them have a sense of time and assist reading days of the week and months of the year.

At Christmas have everyone make at least one gift that is completely handmade for each person in the family.

There's nothing like waking up to my husband lightly strumming his twelve-string guitar, making up new melodies or just practicing favorite tunes in the next room. He's teaching me to play, too, and the hours float by. I love how music fills our days.

Growing up, Saturday was a special day together for my mom and me because my dad and three brothers spent the day at the farm, leaving just the girls to do the chores and shopping for the week—but we'd always sneak in some fun. We could be our truest goofy selves with each other, no grouchy boys to bug or tease us. Now that I'm grown and live six hours from my mama, I miss her the most on Saturdays—so we make a point to call each other early every Saturday morning, sharing our plans for the day and honoring all of our precious times together.

On a rainy day, sit on the porch and watch the rain fall, listen to the thunder, and watch the lightning flash across the sky. Then, forget you are a grown-up and walk right out into it, letting it splash on your face. You can always dry off later.

Find a tree in your yard with low branches and climb up high into it. When you've found a comfortable resting spot, read a book or simply let time pass slowly as you daydream.

Remember how much fun it was to play in the mud as a child? Take your kids to a muddy part of your yard and squish your bare toes through the wet mud. Pay no mind to how dirty you get. Play clothes are replaceable, legs can be washed clean. Memories are forever.

Children greatly enjoy nature. When the air is cool and comfortable and the sun is shining, take a nature hike at a park. Set aside plenty of time and bring a picnic lunch.

When you hear that someone is in need of food or clothes, whether you know them or not, gather together a gift basket for them with necessities and deliver it anonymously.

As a family, make a new tradition of giving to the needy at Christmas and Thanksgiving. Adopt a child or a family, as your budget permits, and give clothes, toys, and food to them. Giving is the quickest way to realize just how blessed you are.

Forget the weight limits on your child's riding toys when your toddler asks you to drive his big fire truck or hop on his Power Wheel's jeep for a ride. The giggles are worth it, and the toy probably won't break!

●

Make dinner special even when children will be at the table. Light the candles, dim the lights, treat your family extra special for no reason at all—except that you love them.

●

Take a hot, steaming bubble bath for as long as it takes you to unwind. Use all the hot water if you need to. Just soak and relax.

●

Buy some decadent, expensive ice cream, plop down in a comfy chair, watch your favorite TV show, and just indulge yourself paying no mind to calories or fat or how much ice cream is left in the carton. You can do that tomorrow.

You know that scene in your favorite soap opera—the one where the man and woman are having a romantic liaison surrounded by a halo of white candles? Go ahead and splurge on the candles. It would be fun just this once.

●

Raking leaves on a crisp sunny fall afternoon doesn't have to be a chore. Once the leaves are raked into a big pile, run as fast as you can right through the middle of them. The thrill is worth having to rake them again.

●

Making a fire outside on a chilly evening is wonderful. The smell of the earthy smoke fills the air and suffuses your clothes. There is no comparison to the warmth of the fire's glow juxtaposed against the cool, crisp night air.

●

Remember the thrill of your first bicycle? You can relive that by riding around the block or down the road a few miles. There is no match for the speed of the pedals beneath your feet and the breeze blowing against your face.

Take advantage of being a passenger in a car on a sunny day. Open the window just enough to let the breeze through as it gently lulls you to a pleasant short nap.

●

Curling up with your dog is something to do every day. If the dog is big, use him as a pillow. If the dog is small, you become the pillow; either way, it's just swell.

●

Warm cinnamon rolls on winter mornings not only fill the air with a fantastic smell, they taste great too!

●

Take your dog to the lake on a hot summer day. She will love playing in the water, and you will find yourself laughing at her crazy antics.

●

Stay in bed just a little longer on a cold winter morning, even after the alarm goes off. Snuggling with the one you love under the warm covers is guaranteed to start your day off right.

Spread a blanket on the grass on a warm spring day for no other reason than to lie down and soak in the warmth, smell, and generous spirit of springtime.

Go on a romantic picnic with your spouse or lover. Bonus points if you ride horses to the spot or take a leisurely outing in a rowboat afterward!

Go out of your way to do one nice thing for a stranger. It could be as simple as holding the door open for someone or volunteering at a homeless shelter. You'd be amazed how much your small actions can help others and yourself.

Take a walk in a meadow on a fresh spring day when the flowers and trees are just beginning to bloom.

Row a boat to a quiet place on the lake and take a lazy nap while the boat is pushed by a gentle breeze.

Call your brother and tell him that you love him.

Take a few minutes and recall the very best day you have ever had. If it was that good, perhaps you should write down all the details so you never forget it.

Show up at your sister's house with a fresh, hot batch of cinnamon buns. And be sure to use the back door. It's friendlier.

Share a peanut-butter-toast breakfast with someone you love.

Make sure an older relative has a few spare blankets in the trunk of her car before winter sets in.

Have a bouquet of balloons delivered to your daughter or niece where she works.

Spend fifteen minutes a day listening to the ones you love. Do nothing else while you listen.

●

Read to your children before bed.

●

Take an elderly person with you when you go antiquing. It's like having your own personal tour guide to the past.

●

Sit a while in the car listening to the rain drum on the roof.

●

Take a long, hot shower by candlelight.

●

As odd and simple as it sounds, I enjoy taking a tennis ball and bouncing it off the side of my brick home for relaxation. When at work, I often sit at my desk and bounce a soft foam-rubber ball against my office wall when I'm working on a mental problem. It relaxes me and lets my mind reset itself.

Have a glass of wine, sit down, and watch a mindless show. In twenty-five minutes, you'll be aching to do something worthwhile or you'll be asleep. Either way, mission accomplished!

●

When the older generation of your family—grandparents, great-aunts and -uncles—are gathered together and start talking about "the good old days," get out a tape recorder or video camera and record the event. It's a fun way to keep your family's history for the next generation.

●

Make a list of all the things you've always wanted to do or just don't do enough. Make a pact with a friend or spouse to check off one activity each month. Refresh your list as new ideas come along. This is one list you don't ever want to finish off.

●

Take a child to the pet store and look at all of the puppies.

Play a board game with your nephew or niece.

Splurge on a brand-new pair of black shoes (even though you have seventy-five pairs in your closet).

Put together a small album of pictures from your favorite vacation. While you're at it, add captions to remember special feelings, places, or memories.

Travel somewhere you've never been before. Go for the extravagant, but settle for the next town over if it qualifies.

Go to a different restaurant when you eat out. Try cuisines from other countries or other regions of your own country.

Visit the old lady next door. Bring her some fresh flowers and listen to her. Just half an hour will make her day.

Do things with your children. Go swimming or take time to play *with* them, rather than just supervising.

●

Spend the afternoon baking and decorating a chocolate cake with your kids.

●

Be there for others who might need you or who would appreciate your thoughtfulness.

●

It is always a good thing to learn a different language, even if it is just the daily stuff. It takes a little time, but about once a week for an hour or two you can learn a lot within three to six months.

●

Gather up as much of your family as possible—across as many generations as you can muster and have each bring a tape or CD with their favorite song and have your own family "music" festival.

Sit down with your preteen child and talk about what her goals are—what kind of job she wants, where she wants to live, whether she will be married or have children. Have her write a letter to herself to be opened sometime in the future, say ten or fifteen years. Keep it in a safe place for her and when the time comes to open it she can then see how she's changed and if she has accomplished her goals.

One thing my husband and I do together is keep the infant nursery on Sunday morning for the early service. We love the kids and we love being together with them!

Encourage someone by sending him a card by post or e-mail. I have a shut-in e-mail friend in Florida, and I do this quite often. She writes me back saying my card of encouragement came at just the right time that she needed it.

Hug your spouse!

With kids grown, and them so busy, take time to phone them. Sometimes my daughter really needs to talk—and we talk for quite a while. Sometimes, even though grown, they need you just to listen to their heart.

This Christmas season, take advantage of the free Christmas concerts and live nativity scenes. It brings into focus the real reason for the season—Jesus's birth.

As I watch my three snow angels, thoughts of warm cocoa and sticky kisses fill my head. The laughter in their tiny voices echoes in my mind. Cold noses and frozen toes are headed my way.

Try a new sport. Take up fly-fishing.

Climb a tall tree as high as you can get. It's most exciting if you can get high enough that the tree sways with your movements!

Well, *I fish and hang out and take vacations and just kind of get away from things. Hang out with my friends that I haven't seen in a long time. And we just kind of just enjoy things. When you play golf and you travel around the world, yeah, that is very enjoyable, but then, again, you are working, too. It is nice to be able to put the sticks down and get away from it and gear back up for it when everything is done.*

—Tiger Woods, golf pro

Give miniatures gaming a try. There are all kinds of options, from faithful military reenactments to fantastic creature battles. Each one offers the chance to improve your tactical skills. Visit your local hobby stores to find out when the next convention is or where a local club meets so you can observe the game a while before investing your time and money in this adventurous pastime.

⚫

Shadow puppets! Design, build, and choreograph your own show for family and friends to enjoy on a summer evening.

⚫

Dig out an old album or cassette (God forbid anyone still owns an eight-track) that used to be a very favorite from high school or the days of romancing your mate. Spend a couple of hours listening for the old memories. Try to appreciate the scratches and tape buzzes that no longer interrupt our listening experience.

On a warm sunny morning, spread out a blanket or towel on the deck or patio. Spend twenty or thirty minutes sitting quietly observing from the inside out.

On a cold blustery morning, spread out a blanket or thick towel near a window. Wrap yourself in another warm blanket, sit quietly, and observe from the inside out.

Sign up to be a room mother or room father. Your children will be very proud.

If you ever played a musical instrument and it has been stuck in a closet or attic for years, dig it out, dust it off, and see if you can still play it. If you dust the piano more than you play it, exercise those fingers for an hour or so. See if the music comes back to you.

On a wintry Friday night the entire family gets together and plans Saturday breakfast. Everyone goes to the grocery and shops for what will be a breakfast to beat all breakfasts. There is only one rule: Everybody has to help on Saturday morning, and that includes cleaning up.

Women seem to love award shows more than men. If that is the case in your house and you want to get a gold star by your name from your wife or girlfriend, fix dinner on Oscar or Grammy night. Serve her dinner during the show. The lights should be low, and be sure to put out candles.

On Thanksgiving morning, give each member of your family a thank-you note. Tell each family member how wonderful they are and why you are so grateful for their love and support.

Your neighbor has a two-month-old baby and she is exhausted. Take dinner over to her house and then baby-sit while she and her husband go to a movie. This won't be a late night. They will be home by 10:00.

A very good friend is getting married and quite a few out-of-town guests are coming. Make your guest room available and volunteer to be a limousine service for the guests.

You have lots and lots of photographs that have never made it into an album. Organize the photos by individuals or families and then make up albums featuring those people or families. Present them with this gift on a special occasion; it is a present that will always be remembered.

This will be a real surprise: Serve your children breakfast in bed. If they are young enough, read a story to them while they are eating.

We have a close-knit family. My grandmother has eight grandchildren and seven great-grandchildren, and we all usually spend Christmas together. Over the course of a year, my cousins and I gathered photos of our children to present to her in an album at Christmastime. Each family added personal touches to the final book. She enjoyed receiving it, and I hope she'll enjoy it for years to come.

Bike riding is fun, but it is not risk free. Saturday mornings are a perfect time to teach your child bicycle safety. This should be fun and it gives you great one-on-one time.

You have a new neighbor or coworker who is single and from out of town. Introduce him or her to your eligible friends.

Also, invite him or her over to your house for dinner.

It dawns on you that you have a little extra time on your hands. Freeze several homemade casseroles and take them over to an elderly friend who would consider your visit and your dinners to be a real treat.

•

Every family has a mother, father, brother, or sister who can never remember important dates. Fill out a calendar with all of those dates and then give it to your absentminded relative. This is something you might have to do every year.

•

Gather up your family or group of friends and sign up for a bird-watching hike.

•

Don't know how to ride a bike? There's no time like the present! There are probably plenty of graduating seniors at your local college or university who are willing to part with their bikes pretty cheaply.

Whenever you hear about a friend or relative being promoted, send a congratulations card.

●

Take an overnight biking trip with a group of friends or family members. Of course you'll be sore, but there are plenty of trails where even unpracticed, haven't-ridden-a-bike-since-grade-school types can keep up with the rest of the pack. You really will enjoy it.

●

You know that thing that's sitting in your garage or basement that you had to have at the time? The one that cost you over three hundred dollars but hasn't seen much use since that first week? Whether it's an exercise machine, a woodworking tool, or a recreational vehicle, you must make a decision. Either work it into your weekly or monthly routine, or get rid of it!

●

Memorize a love poem and surprise your spouse by reciting it during a candlelit dinner.

Lots of people have collections of things, whether valuable or not, that they're not willing to part with. It will be a much more pleasing collection if you organize it and invest in some way to display it, making it a part of your house or office décor instead of clutter in the background.

Buy (or build if you are handy) two or three birdhouses and place them strategically around the yard. These will give you and your family pleasure month after month, year after year.

Clean out and wash your spouse's car. Then fill it up and have the oil changed.

Do something memorable for your in-laws that includes you and your spouse. (Giving them a two-week vacation doesn't count.) Take them on a hot-air balloon ride. Arrange for a carriage ride and a picnic. Make them dinner with all of their favorite foods. Go to a bookstore, do a little browsing, and then treat them to a book of their choice.

Elderly neighbors often need a little help. Pick up their newspaper and place it by the front door. Help them with heavy lifting. Shovel the snow for them. Go to the grocery for them.

Let's assume you have been out of school for a while. You can really brighten the day of one of your old teachers by sending a thank-you note. Be sure to tell him why you think he was so good.

Your video camera is meant to be used. Make it a point to get your parents on tape. Ask them lots and lots of questions about their parents, their friends, their childhood memories, their dreams, their fears, their concerns, and anything that comes to mind. Think of it as recording a great conversation.

Write down some of your beliefs about religion, family, work, sports, movies, books, and so on, and then share them with your family.

Keep in touch with your old friends. Send letters, pictures of your children, e-mails, and addresses and phone numbers of mutual friends.

*

Make a list of new clothes that your spouse really needs but is hesitating to buy for himself or herself. Without any warning, take your spouse by the hand, get in the car, and tell him/her that you are going shopping.

*

Go to a baseball game *really* early with your son and two or three of his best friends. Watch batting and fielding practice, walk all around the stadium, buy a souvenir, try to get an autograph or two, eat hot dogs and Crackerjacks, and cheer for the home team.

*

Ice skating on a local pond in the deep of winter with a nearby bonfire to warm up by provides the perfect backdrop for a lifetime of fond memories. If you don't have ice skates, put on some rubber boots instead. I have it on good authority that they work just as well on good solid ice.

If it's an option where you live, try your hand at ice fishing. As with many things, you must prepare well, or you may regret the decision to do it.

*

Have you ever known or been a snow bunny? Plan a weekend at a ski resort to discover or rediscover the exhilaration of downhill skiing.

*

Take the time to savor winter by not being afraid of it and the cold. Go snow camping. Show shoes; waterproof, insulated clothing; and a book on how to build and fortify a snow cave to sleep in with your son or daughter. Try it in the backyard or city park first. You'll find a snow cave mighty warm, very cozy, and perfect after a long day of watching winter droop from tree boughs.

*

Try backpacking in a foreign country. Youth hostels abound in Western Europe. Pack lightly, and take advantage of the generally open culture.

I know a few people who apprenticed or studied in a winery or restaurant abroad. If you're just beginning (or beginning again) in the food industry, this is an option well worth your investigation. You may also come away from the experience with another language in your repertoire.

●

Take a trip on the ocean to go whale spotting.

●

Try deep-sea fishing one summer, or better yet, during a spring or fall.

●

Make a list of all the foreign countries you'd like to visit. Do some research to make sure you're certain of your destination, then whittle the list until it is manageable. Make a commitment to travel with your spouse or a good friend to one of the places every five years—or more often if you can manage it.

"Rustic" transport, such as the train, is convenient for travel among Western European destinations, usually at a lower rate than airfare, and more picturesque.

*

Foreign travel doesn't have to cost nearly as much as you might think. With a little research, you can plan trips abroad for a lot less. Options such as air courier don't leave much room for luggage, but you can usually plan ahead, and it's a lot easier on your pocketbook than full fare when you're considering traveling to Eastern Europe or Asia. Subscribe to *The Shoestring Traveler* or join the International Association of Air Travel Couriers to keep up to date on courier travel options.

*

I may be biased, but I believe there are very few people out there who don't enjoy a good meal. Take a cooking class to learn a new cuisine or even how to boil vegetables properly! Even if you are an accomplished cook, there's something out there for you.

Books are great for light entertainment or research, but they can serve in a pinch for a vacation, too. Where do you feel like traveling this week? Find a novel or nonfiction account about that place, whether it's a farm in Wisconsin or the Comoros islands. Prepare your reading place with appropriate accessories as available—go overboard with life vest, oars, and a heat lamp for the Comoros!—and keep plenty of beverages at your disposal. You're in for the long haul.

•

One Saturday, agree to put the television remote control away where it can't be used for the entire day. By the end of the day, you will either watch television much differently or you will think the inventor of the remote control was a genius!

•

Make plans with friends to go canoeing. Children are optional.

My husband and I participate in an annual cookout on Memorial Day with our friends. Everyone brings some food and an outdoor game, and we go to a local park to cook and play. We love it, because the only cleanup involved is tossing paper plates and napkins into a barrel!

When the kids are old enough to cooperate but not old enough to protest, take a road trip vacation. Once you decide the general direction you're going, everyone gets to pick a destination, such as the largest ball of string, a well-known museum, or a hiking campsite. Take a cooler and picnic basket, and this doesn't have to be expensive at all!

My spouse and I enjoy entertaining friends at our house once a month or more. Sometimes we prepare food, and sometimes we just provide games and entertainment. We almost always welcome kids, and it's usually a relaxing, fun time for everyone.

Start going to church or synagogue again.

Keep a monthly or even weekly luncheon date with your girlfriends, or just with your best friend—the one you've known since childhood and wouldn't want to live without.

•

Poker night. Make it a ritual that must be observed in your household. After all, everyone needs his space, especially dads with young children. Just make it a point to trade off nights with your spouse so she can get her girl time in, too.

•

Spend a good half a day at the nearest amusement park with your children.

•

On your next anniversary, relive your first date with your spouse, or come as close as you can get. Request the same table, if you remember which one it was, and pretend you have to get to know each other all over again. It may even jump-start your relationship!

Get out a "gonna." Both my mother and grandmother had gonnas. These were craft or sewing projects that they had started or practically finished that were for various reasons relegated to a box or a basket before completion. I had a gonna at the tender age of nine or ten. I had learned to cross-stitch and chose pillowcases as a project. My mom helped me with the little iron-on pattern, and set me up with needle, thread, and an embroidery hoop. I completed one pillowcase and nearly completed the mate when life got busy or I discovered the joy in other activities, thus ending my interest in the project. But since I had nearly completed the set of pillowcases I couldn't bear the thought of throwing them out. These pillowcases were packed away in a Jones Store folding shirt box, along with the thread, needle, and hoop.

This was my gonna. Every so often I would come across that box, having forgotten what was in it, and open it up to discover my gonna. Then I'd say to myself something I'd heard my mother and grandmother say many times.

"Someday I'm gonna finish that project." As an adult I did finally finish those pillowcases. One gonna down, and plenty of others to go.

I'm afraid when my mother passes on I'll be the recipient of many of her gonnas, and some that she graciously claimed when her mother passed away. With the intent of finishing them, of course.

**—Jennifer Underwood,
administrative assistant and yoga instructor**

Clean out your closets. If you're like most people I know, you should set aside a whole weekend for this. Not only will you find things to throw out or to give away, but you'll also reconnect with bits of your past, as you sift through your "junk pile" to separate the wheat from the chaff.

●

Regarding that "garage sale" pile in your house or garage: Throw out the junk, and give away the rest unless you have an actual date marked on your calendar. It's a rare garage or yard sale that's really worth the time and effort you put into it, and the space you're devoting to it in the meantime is just a cluttered mess.

●

Participate in a neighborhood yard sale. It's a good way to get rid of the idle baby and children's toys, chairs, and so on, that are taking up perfectly good space in your teenager's closet.

Do you often mutter "Sunday drivers" under your breath? Try it yourself. On a lazy Sunday, take a leisurely drive on some country back roads that you're vaguely familiar with. Go slow, roll down the windows, and enjoy the fresh air.

All parents must do it at least once: Take the whole family to Disneyland or Disney World for a couple days of very expensive, but quite good, fun.

Take the opportunity Halloween provides to make a pumpkin pie completely from scratch. It's an involved process, but at least you'll be able to say you did it once!

Go all out one Halloween and make a spooky scene inside your house. Don't give away any candy until the local spooks have felt your bowls of peeled grape eyeballs and spaghetti innards and been scared by at least one accomplice dressed as a creepy witch.

Buy a book or call your park service to find out where you can find a nice, long hiking trail. Get prepared like a good Boy Scout, then take a friend or go alone, but go.

Volunteer with your local 4-H group. There is so much work to be done in a community that takes its 4-H seriously!

Go camping in some actual wilderness, where you leave your TV, air-conditioning, and shower behind, and where you have to gather your own firewood, sleep in a bedroll, and perhaps even forage for some of your food. You won't be gone from civilization that long, anyway, and you may find yourself relaxing as you let go your concerns about "that report due next week." Hint: no laptops or cell phones allowed.

Donate a year of your spare time to the Boy or Girl Scout troop of your choice. It's easiest, of course, when your own children are involved, but there is almost always room for an extra den mother or scout leader when the intentions are good.

During a spring or summer rainstorm, open what windows you can without letting in the storm, lie down on a couch or bed, and just listen to the rain on the roof and relax.

On a hot summer day when the neighborhood kids are out playing, break out a whole box of ice pops to share with them.

One of the best things about summer nights: the ice cream truck's music coming up a nearby street.

Set your alarm clock for 4:30 A.M. one Wednesday. Brew and enjoy a cup of hot tea or coffee, take a morning walk alone, and enjoy the dewy mist of the breaking morning before you go in to take your shower and attack the day.

Take a trip to New York and grab a smothered hot dog from a street vendor.

Take the time to walk in a new stretch of woods or on a country road with your loved ones. The sense of discovery and the restorative power of nature will invigorate you and teach you new things about yourself and your family members.

Take a moment to call a brother or sister with whom you have a rocky relationship. Don't wait for him or her to come around to your way of thinking. Regard his or her views as personal, and yours as the ones you can change. I began to feel more comfortable around my family after years of feeling out of place. It dawned on me that they hadn't changed; I had.

Especially if your children are teenagers, call a family meeting as soon as possible. It's a good way to find out what your family members have been up to and what's coming up, and it's great face-to-face time. In fact, I recommend having family meetings at least once a month. You can spice it up by following it up with a night out at your family's favorite restaurant or catching a movie matinee together.

Take your teenager out with you on a Saturday afternoon. You can have brunch, do some shopping, and see a matinee. All good entertainments for both of you, they amount to a day of one-on-one parent-child time—and end before her friends are ready to go out for the night!

Buy some face paint and do a little artwork on your children's and your own face, then all of you go out for dinner and let people wonder what you are up to.

Spend the afternoon playing Barbie dolls with your daughter.

Have your children tell you about a typical day at school for them in great detail. They'll love to talk about their routine and you will enjoy finding out about it.

Share a bag of Oreo cookies and a jug of milk with your kids after a hard day of work and learning.

Buy a cowboy hat and tickets for the rodeo!

Stay up all night and listen to the Art Bell radio show. You can't possibly begin to imagine the strange people who live in this world until you've done this one time.

Tonight for dinner, prepare something that no one in your home has ever tasted before. If it turns out to be good, so much the better. If it turns out awful, chalk it up as a lesson.

Watch a live presentation of *West Side Story*. A talented cast of singers and dancers will make this classic worth seeing again and again.

Some people have a goal to attend at least one of sport's "big four"—the Kentucky Derby, the Indianapolis 500, the Super Bowl, and the World Series. Perhaps you should, too?

●

If you have never ridden a motorcycle, perhaps *now* is the time to give it a whirl?

●

How long has it been since you created anything using papier-mâché? Sure, it makes a mess, but that's just a part of the fun.

●

Organize with a neighbor (or two) to take turns hauling newspapers, glass, cans, and plastics to a recycling center once a month.

●

Compile enough information on an older relative so you can send it to your local newspaper on a big event like a fiftieth wedding anniversary or a ninetieth birthday, and so on.

Instead of throwing away your *Reader's Digest* and other monthly magazines when you are finished with them, take them to a hospital waiting room and leave them for others to help pass what could be a very difficult time.

On your way to the dry cleaner's this week stop by an aged neighbor's house to see if you can take anything for her with you or run an errand for her while you're out.

Invite a friend out for a game of darts.

Next time you are in the mood to bake a cake, make two or three and drop the extras off at a local firehouse. The firefighters will think you're an angel and you'll be glad you did!

Try this: Invite a few close friends over for fondue by candlelight and watch the Cary Grant and Ginger Rogers classic *Once Upon a Honeymoon.*

This Labor Day weekend stay up the entire time with Jerry Lewis and watch the stars come out.

●

On a hot July afternoon do a little Christmas shopping—it never hurts to start early!

●

If you've never done it, go ahead—order something online. You'll have to jump on the Internet wagon sooner or later. Might as well be sooner.

●

Don't miss the opportunity for Take Our Daughters to Work day when it rolls around this year.

●

Spend a few moments each day for a week writing down the names of every relative whom you can remember. It may set you on a course of discovery of your own heritage.

●

At least one time on your life you must plan a trip to NASA on the Space Coast of Florida to watch an actual launch. It is an awesome display of power and technology.

Sleep! Sleeping is big fun because I get really burned out. My brain can do only so many things at once, and I have to recoup. My idea of heaven is to lounge and luxuriate in bed, and not have to get up, just kind of roll around in nice, clean, soft sheets with lots of pillows and have my little dog up there with me. And if there's a pile of catalogs, all the better.

—Delta Burke, actress

You know that guy who stands out front of McDonald's with the sign, "Will Work for Food"? Next time you pick up a sandwich, pick up one for him. Your act of kindness will fill an empty belly for a few hours, and may inspire kindness in others.

Spend time today working out a few secret phrases with your spouse or companion. The next time you are with others and one of you says, "The weather sure has been balmy lately," that could be your secret message to your spouse that means, "Let's get out of here, quick!"

Call or write your best friend today. Friends are so important that we shouldn't take them for granted. Ralph Waldo Emerson said, "A friend may well be reckoned the masterpiece of nature." Henry Durbanville made this observation about friendship: "A friend is the first person to come in when the whole world goes out."

Rummage through the attic to find your old baseball cards and the memories that seeing them again will bring back.

•

Host a birthday party at your place for a grandchild, niece, or nephew.

•

On the next New Year write down all of your resolutions, hopes, goals, and dreams for the coming year. Have your children do the same then put those papers in a coffee can and bury it in the backyard. On the following New Year's Eve dig up the can and review its contents with your family.

•

Find a copy of your favorite poem and learn it well enough so that you can recite it from memory.

•

Determine to have a personal tradition. Whether it's cooked cabbage every New Year's Day, opening Christmas presents a day early, or attending every opening-day baseball game—you need your very own tradition.

Picking and eating green apples right off the tree is one of those little joys that make summertime special.

*

A friend once told me that her very favorite childhood memory was her dad coming home from work late at night with a Hershey's chocolate bar just for her. The two would share a dance, her standing on Daddy's feet. Lifetime memories don't have to be expensive; in fact, the best ones never are.

*

Do you remember holding hands, your first kiss, and the first movie you saw together? Perhaps you should relive those memories with your love tonight.

*

Aren't you glad you live in America, where you can still play stickball under the streetlights until midnight?

*

When was the last time you hand-beat egg whites for meringue? Just because you can buy it made doesn't mean you shouldn't do it the old-fashioned way now and again!

Been traveling for work too much lately? Burn the frequent-flier miles and take your kids with you to someplace they want to go. Better yet, make it really special and take them one at a time.

●

You know, you can put peanuts in your glass of Coke at home and no one but you will ever know.

●

On a hot summer day a family water fight can be more fun than a trip to the pool.

●

There really is little reason to own a convertible if on a warm summer day you don't go to a drive-in root beer stand and have a few chili dogs with a frosty mug of root beer.

●

Does your town still have an ice cream parlor? Today would be a good day to visit it.

●

Visit a local dairy and get a really fresh gallon or two of milk to go.

Organize a game of Wiffle ball in the backyard and don't be surprised if it lasts until well after sunset. That's when the game gets good!

Sitting in front of the fireplace cracking hickory nuts for homemade fudge is a wonderful way to spend a frosty Saturday afternoon.

Do you remember sitting on your grandmother's front porch with your brother, sister, or cousin, and snapping green beans for canning? Plant a garden this year and make some new memories with your own children or grandchildren.

Getting older doesn't mean you can't still be a kid . . . but it *does* mean that you can now afford to build the very best treehouse in the neighborhood!

Find a place where you can still buy a fountain cherry Coke—like the ones we used to get at the Woolworth lunch counter—and you've found a treasure.

Who hasn't stood barefoot in the freshly mown grass on a warm sunny day and spun around and around until they were dizzy? It's never too late to give it a whirl.

Hang your sheets outside to dry this week. The smell of fresh bedsheets late at night is worth the extra effort.

Sunday afternoon, after church and dinner, why not curl up on the couch with some warm cashews and the comic section of the newspaper? Add a fuzzy warm comforter and a quality nap is sure to follow!

Organize a neighborhood softball game and don't forget to bring along several ice-cold watermelons.

Cut out paper dolls with your daughter, niece, or granddaughter and then dress them with cut-out clothes from the Sears catalog. You both will cherish that time together.

Play hide-and-seek outside around sundown—but watch out for the mosquitoes!

Put a clean bucket in the backyard during the next rain shower to collect enough water to wash and rinse your hair with rainwater.

Pick up several audio books on tape or CD for those long, boring commutes. The time will pass so much faster.

If you don't already have one, volunteer to take on the task of compiling the family info book. Get the postal address, phone number, and e-mail address of all your known relatives, put it into one document, and mail it to everyone in your family.

Put together a list of your own family traditions that you'd like to see passed down for future generations.

A sailboat ride on a bright summer day will exhilarate and refresh your tired old bones.

Do you ever wonder about your ancestors and how life was for them? Since you are your descendants' ancestor, perhaps you should write a special message to be viewed seventy-five or even a hundred years from now by your own descendants.

●

Take a leisure walk around your neighborhood, stopping to chat with any neighbor who might be so inclined.

●

Start your crop of tomato plants indoors in the early spring for transplanting outside when it gets warmer. You'll have a jump on the growing season.

●

If you enjoy golf, you should make plans to someday play Pebble Beach. Not only is it said to be one of the most challenging venues, but it also boasts an invigorating and dramatic backdrop of coastline.

●

Get your hands on the local newspaper for the day of your birth and take a look at how things were in your world back then. A library near you will likely have a stash of microfilm or microfiche that you can browse.

Assemble the NCAA basketball brackets for all the teams in the "Big Dance" this year. Have everyone in your house make their picks prior to the start of the tournament and see who in your family is the college basketball expert. If you're so inclined, winner doesn't do any chores for a month!

Volunteer to "cook" dinner tonight by bringing home Chinese takeout. With a deal like that you could even volunteer to do the dishes!

Buy a pack of limited time long-distance calling cards and include one with Christmas, birthday, and other cards that you send.

Drag your family (and the dog) to the photographer to make pictures for this year's Christmas cards.

Ride your bicycle to the library for an afternoon of fun and fiction.

Treat yourself to a new pair of tennis shoes. Everyone steps a little livelier in a new pair of "kicks."

Recording your favorite TV shows frees you up in two ways: You don't have to sit in front of the TV if you're not in the mood; and, presto!—you now have something worth watching on those evenings when there's just nothing good on television.

The little ones seem to like to "camp out" in the family room by putting a blanket over a couple of chairs, creating a makeshift tent. You'll be their hero if you let them do it sometime.

Visit one of the many decommissioned naval vessels in ports around the country. It's amazing that so many people could live and work in such cramped quarters—and with such military success!

Sometime during summer vacation, ask your child to do a short report about space. She can pick any aspect of it, from plain old science to historic space exploration to fantasy space travel. Allow use of the Internet, but encourage a visit to the library, too. You may awaken a desire in a future astronaut!

Rummage through your and your spouse's jewelry boxes, and finally take all your watches with run-down batteries to the jewelry store for new batteries!

Organize a neighborhood dance or party—in costume—at a large local barn for Halloween next year. If you live in a city, improvise and rent a small warehouse! Decorate with plenty of hay bales.

Send your children on an old-fashioned hayride this fall. Many small farms on the outskirts of towns make such rides available for just a few dollars, and they often include a pumpkin patch or a petting zoo, too.

Volunteer to organize the haunted house or forest for your teenager's friends this year. Include their parents in the planning, and you'll get to know them at the same time you're providing safe entertainment for the kids.

Seek out a salt-water pool and let your body relax in the warmth of the brine.

Planning a day at the amusement park for the sole purpose of scaring yourself silly on the roller coaster is okay. Screaming at the top of your lungs while plunging down the hill with your hands raised in the air is okay. Throwing up on fellow riders is *not* okay. Got it?

For a bit of international flavor, learn to play snooker.

Listen to the sounds of the ocean. Even if you have to buy a CD with the sound of the sea, the sound of the ebb and flow of the tide is reassuring and will bring much contentment to your soul.

Kickboxing aerobics is a great way to exercise and take out your frustrations without getting arrested.

When the weather doesn't cooperate for some planned outdoor activity, try just sitting by the window with some tea, put your feet up, and just close your eyes and think about all the wonderful things in your life.

Enjoy a long, hot steam bath at your local health club or spa.

Spend a cool summer evening swinging on the front porch watching the cars drive by. That sounds pretty boring—so try it with your spouse and snuggle a little. See, isn't that much better?

Visit a hot mineral spring and soak in the steamy, bubbling waters from deep within the earth.

Make an educational trip to a science center or natural history museum somewhere near your home. Such an adventure is worth taking the kids out of school for the day!

Spend the afternoon with your closest friend discussing at length all those things you can't normally talk about—religion, politics, abortion, whether or not there are aliens. Anything that isn't politically correct is fair game for this session.

Spend the day protesting something. Go to a march. Make signs. Take a petition around the neighborhood for a cause in which you are really indignant.

Make tonight a Great Wall night at your house. Stir-fry in your own wok and put kung-fu reruns on the tube.

Movie night with the gang: The night of the next premiere you're all (or nearly all) excited about, get together early enough with your buddies to have a long dinner and catch up before the movie.

Add some incentive to your health walks. Select a place where you have always wanted to visit. Calculate the mileage from your house to that location. Once you've logged that many miles on your health walk, reward your diligence with a trip there!

Take a reading vacation this year. Bring all the books you think you can stand and then bring a few more. Spend nearly the entire time doing nothing but reading—reading on the beach, in the hotel room, at the restaurant while waiting on dinner. Catch up on all that reading that you never seem to have time for.

Sleep in late; put on your friendliest pair of Levi's with a sweatshirt and no socks or shoes. Don't comb your hair, answer the phone, or do any dishes. This is *your* one guilt-free, lazy-as-you-want-it-to-be day for this year!

To a large pan, add plenty of marbles (at least cover the bottom), 1/2 cup salt, *hot* water (as hot as you can stand), seven to ten drops of lavender and citrus essential oils. Soak your feet in the pan while rolling them on the marbles. Say "Ahhhhh."

I can't play the first note on a piano but that doesn't mean that I don't enjoy banging away on one from time to time.

An afternoon of racquetball with a friend will really get your blood pumping and make you sleep like a baby that night.

Someday when they least expect it, take your children out of school for a day. Take only one child at a time, and do something special—lunch out, shopping, a movie, a long walk, an amusement park, the beach. It'll be a mini-vacation for just the two of you.

Spend the afternoon in a sunny corner of your local library. Look at books you wouldn't normally come across and enjoy the astounding collection of words.

Every grandparent, aunt, or uncle worth their salt has a penny drawer—a place filled with pennies where little hands get a free grab when visiting. You'd better start collecting your spare change now for the next visit!

Take a morning bike ride while the grass is still wet with dew to McDonald's for an early-morning breakfast.

This year, why not have an Easter egg hunt in your backyard?

Organize a play date for your young children.

Pick up a box of encouragement cards. Make it a goal to send one out a week to your family, friends, and neighbors until the cards are gone. Your thoughtfulness will be much appreciated.

Assemble a logbook for your vehicles. Include maintenance information, gasoline purchased, and miles driven. It's a great way to keep tabs on your transportation costs and track the efficiency of your autos, and it might even come in handy at tax time.

Find out the Blue Book values on all your vehicles this weekend. It's always good to know those numbers well in advance of looking for a new car.

Surprise your spouse with a kid-free night. Plan ahead for a baby-sitter who can watch them away from your home so you and your spouse can be alone in the house for once.

A moonlit drive in the country on a warm summer evening is a romantic ending to a perfect day.

Buy a few gift certificates for a movie and a snack at your favorite theater; they make the perfect impromptu gift when you need one. If it goes unused for a long time, treat yourself to it!

A steaming cup of cherry white mocha java and your favorite magazine is a wonderful accompaniment while you wait out an afternoon rain shower.

●

Pack a picnic basket with lunch for two and surprise your spouse at work when you show up for lunch at the office.

●

Round up all the unused eyeglasses around your house and donate them to one of the many places that put them to good use. You can even organize an eyeglasses drive at work. Your coworkers can bring theirs to the office to add to your donation.

●

Houseboating is an easy way for families or friends to vacation on the water. With an hour or less of on-the-spot instruction, even novice boaters are set for one of the most relaxing vacations imaginable.

●

Set up your vacation slides and enjoy them the way they were intended—alone with a TV dinner!

I *like puttering; I like several different projects going on at the same time: something down in my garage on the bench, organizing a shelf, doing some paperwork, watching TV, and then thinking about what I'm going to eat. All in one Saturday. That's a great day to me. Probably, right now, my favorite stuff to mess around with is my video equipment or my computer. I'm constantly turning the computer on, fooling around with it, blowing it up, and then coming back to it. I don't really do much with it, but it's a fascinating machine.*

—Tim Allen, actor

How about a wash, cut, and style before having a bowl of cold cucumber soup at your favorite lunch spot?

Give an outrageously excessive tip for excellent service at a restaurant.

Visit a war memorial and spend some time reflecting on your freedom, which was bought with blood.

Go ahead, I dare you—announce your best friend's birthday with a large spot in your local paper and be sure to include a corny old high school photo!

Tell someone you love to quit smoking today. It is a matter of life and death.

Write "I Love You" in the windshield frost of your wife's car one morning when you leave before her!

Read *On Gold Mountain* by Lisa See.

Clear some time one Saturday morning to sit down with your spouse and review your retirement finances. If you find you need help, seek the advice of a professional financial planner.

•

Spend an entire day consciously trying to put your "best face forward." Smile at strangers on the street; thank the salespersons, cashiers, and others who provide services for you; hug your spouse and children a little longer; spread compliments liberally to your coworkers, friends, and family; and be courteous to the telemarketers (just this once).

•

Use that change in your pocket to pick up an extra soda for a coworker when you go for a refill. Do not accept repayment!

•

When you land that big account, don't just go to a bar; take everyone to an inexpensive game of hockey or soccer instead. There's still plenty of beer available, and they need the fan support.

Get to know your next-door neighbors by hosting a dinner party. You may want to share phone numbers so you'll each be available if you need advice or help when you're on vacation.

Make a gift of a tool kit to a single woman. Everybody needs a hammer, a few screwdrivers, and an adjustable wrench on occasion!

Do you have a good pair of sunglasses, a variety of fresh batteries, a reliable watch, a loaded camera, a supply of lightbulbs, a current road atlas, an extra toothbrush, Scotch tape, super glue, and a complete first aid kit? If you're missing any of these, go to a general store and stock up!

Buy a filing cabinet for your home files. Spend a morning organizing the bills, health records, bank statements, and other important personal information for your family.

When we were all still young enough to count as children, our parents would get us together to shuck the sweet corn they'd planted with the field corn that year. We'd take shifts all morning. One group would shuck the corn from the truck bed, fresh from the field, handing the ears off to the next group who would then pick off the "silks" until they were clean enough even for Kevin (you know who you are!). When we had a good bunch ready to go, another group was waiting in the kitchen to blanch and cut the corn for freezing—jobs usually reserved for Granny and our moms—but we would help bag the steaming corn (and we took the opportunity to sample the goods). Shucks, silks, and empty cobs would go to the pigs for slop.

To make this work in your household, plant a few rows of corn in your garden, enlist the kids and some of their friends to help when it's time to harvest, and add the "slop" to your compost heap for next year's garden. And here's a hint: Freshly cut sweet corn is so good it doesn't need butter to melt in your mouth!

—Kelly Gilbert, editor and mom

Go through all the underwear drawers in the house. Toss out all too-small and worn garments and replace them with new ones. Your family will thank you.

·

Rock your baby to sleep tonight.

·

Take your preteen to the library and don't leave until he's found at least two books to read at home.

·

Clear out your linen closet and launder everything that hasn't been used for a year before putting it back in.

·

Change all the sheets in the house this weekend. Let everybody have a fresh start to the new week in crisp bed linens!

·

During a thunderstorm turn off all the lights in your house and stretch out where you can enjoy nature's light show through a window.

Take a picnic lunch to a municipal park during the middle of the week when there won't be many parents and children there. Your kids will be excited to have the park nearly to themselves. Don't forget your novel, either, because this is their day, and if you get restless you may be tempted to leave early.

•

After securing permission from the teacher, drop in on your child's class one day with refreshments. You'll be a hero for a day!